CAMBRIDGE
Global English
Activity Book

Jane Boylan and Claire Medwell

CAMBRIDGE
UNIVERSITY PRESS

CAMBRIDGE
UNIVERSITY PRESS

University Printing House, Cambridge CB2 8BS, United Kingdom

Cambridge University Press is part of the University of Cambridge.

It furthers the University's mission by disseminating knowledge in the pursuit of education, learning and research at the highest international levels of excellence.

Information on this title: education.cambridge.org

© Cambridge University Press 2014

This publication is in copyright. Subject to statutory exception and to the provisions of relevant collective licensing agreements, no reproduction of any part may take place without the written permission of Cambridge University Press.

First published 2014
8th printing 2016

Printed in India by Multivista Global Pvt Ltd

A catalogue record for this publication is available from the British Library

ISBN 978-1-107-62686-7 Paperback

Cambridge University Press has no responsibility for the persistence or accuracy of URLs for external or third-party internet websites referred to in this publication, and does not guarantee that any content on such websites is, or will remain, accurate or appropriate.

CD 1	
Learner's Book	
Track number on CD	Track number in book
1	1
2	2
3	3
4	4
5	5
6	6
7	7
8	8
9	9
10	10
11	11
12	12
13	13
14	14
15	15
16	16
17	17
18	18
19	19
20	20
21	21
22	22
23	23
24	24
25	25
26	26
27	27
28	28
29	29
30	30
31	31
32	32

CD 2					
Learner's Book					
Track number on CD	Track number in book		Track number on CD	Track number in book	
1	33		**Activity Book**		
2	34		29	61	
3	35		30	62	
4	36		31	63	
5	37		32	64	
6	38		33	65	
7	39		34	66	
8	40		35	67	
9	41		36	68	
10	42		37	69	
11	43		38	70	
12	44		39	71	
13	45		40	72	
14	46		41	73	
15	47		42	74	
16	48		43	75	
17	49		44	76	
18	50		45	77	
19	51		46	78	
20	52		47	79	
21	53		48	80	
22	54				
23	55				
24	56				
25	57				
26	58				
27	59				
28	60				

Contents

UNIT 1 Life experience
1 Free-time activities — 4
2 A first time for everything — 6
3 Inspiring people — 8
4 Extraordinary experiences — 10
5 An inspiring life — 12
6 Unit 1 Revision — 14
    My global progress — 15

UNIT 2 School
1 My school day — 16
2 What is brain power? — 18
3 A problem shared — 20
4 Starting something new — 22
5 Classroom politics — 24
6 Unit 2 Revision — 26
    My global progress — 27

UNIT 3 Sport
1 Get active — 28
2 Yes I can — 30
3 Giving instructions — 32
4 Marathon achievement — 34
5 Football crazy — 36
6 Unit 3 Revision — 38
    My global progress — 39

UNIT 4 The big screen
1 Describing films — 40
2 The first movies — 42
3 What makes a good film? — 44
4 Creating film scenes — 46
5 Spectacular special effects — 48
6 Unit 4 Revision — 50
    My global progress — 51

UNIT 5 Inventions
1 Gadgets — 52
2 Great minds — 54
3 Bright ideas — 56
4 Changing the world — 58
5 Believe in yourself — 60
6 Unit 5 Revision — 62
    My global progress — 63

UNIT 6 Explorers
1 On a mission! — 64
2 Exploration exploits — 66
3 Intrepid explorers — 68
4 Keeping track — 70
5 Big adventures — 72
6 Unit 6 Revision — 74
    My global progress — 75

UNIT 7 Jobs and work
1 Just the job! — 76
2 The joy is in the job — 78
3 Designing a uniform — 80
4 Looking for a job — 82
5 Achieving a goal — 84
6 Unit 7 Revision — 86
    My global progress — 87

UNIT 8 Communication
1 Ways of communicating — 88
2 Getting the message — 90
3 Explaining something difficult — 92
4 Getting your point across — 94
5 A thank you letter — 96
6 Unit 8 Revision — 98
    My global progress — 99

UNIT 9 Travellers' tales
1 Have a go! — 100
2 Where shall we go? — 102
3 Describing a special place — 104
4 My dream holiday — 106
5 Other kinds of journeys — 108
6 Unit 9 Revision — 110
    My global progress — 111

1 Life experience

1 Free-time activities

1 Vocabulary Activities
Complete the speech bubbles with the correct form of the verbs from the box.

take photos
play video games
play the piano
painting
meet up with my friends
~~play football~~

a I really like ¹ _playing football_ every week. with my big brother. He's been in the school team for three years now and can teach me a lot.

b I definitely prefer creative activities to sports. I'm hopeless at sport. Maybe that's why I don't like it. I love ²_____, and sometimes I go out and ³_____ of wild animals for my pictures. I'm quite good at photography – last year I won a prize at school.

c I don't have much free time at the moment. I ⁴_____ most nights after school. I have to practise a lot because I'm training for a national music competition.

d Most weekends I ⁵_____ . We ⁶_____ together if the weather is bad and we can't go outside. If the weather is OK, we go out on our bikes. I can't stand being outside when it's cold and raining – I hate it!

2 Word study Preferences
Underline the eight phrases in Activity 1 that describe preferences and abilities.

3 Use of English *Wh-* question forms review
Make questions using the words below. Which response (a–d) from Activity 1 answers each question?

> **Use of English**
>
> **Wh- questions review**
> **Question word** + **do** + **you** + verb? + ?
> What do you like doing when you've got some free time?
> **Who do you** spend your free time with?
> **Which** places **do you** like going to?

1 you / much / free time / do / how / have? _____
   How much free time do you have?
   Response: _____

2 at the weekends / do / what / you / do? _____
   _____
   Response: _____

3 playing / do / who / you / football / like / with? _____
   _____
   Response: _____

4 prefer / which / you / do / activities? _____
   _____
   Response: _____

4 Word study Preferences
Make true sentences about your own preferences for free-time activities.

1 I prefer _____ to _____ .
2 I'm quite _____ at _____ .
3 I'm hopeless _____ _____ .
4 I _____ like _____ .
5 I don't _____ .
6 I _____ stand _____ .

5 📝 **Challenge**

Think of a famous person you like. Imagine you're going to interview this person. Write four questions to ask him/her. Then imagine his/her responses and write them down.

Cambridge Global English Stage 6 Activity Book Unit 1 5

2 A first time for everything

Strategy check! Understanding general meaning
Tick the strategies which will help you to understand general meaning.
Use the strategies before you read the text below.

- Look for key words in a text. ☐
- Read the whole text in detail. ☐
- Look at pictures or headings. ☐
- Look up all the words you don't understand. ☐

1 **Read** about these first-time experiences. Match a comment to a picture.

1 'I tried rock climbing last year for the first time (in a sports centre, not outside on real rocks!). I've always been afraid of heights but I decided to have a go. It was **amazing**! Afterwards I felt very **satisfied** because I'd done something **brave**!' *Callum, 12*

2 'The first time I saw an elephant, I was **terrified**! In my country, it is quite normal to see elephants in the countryside, but I had never seen anything like it before. Now I think elephants are **beautiful**.' *Sumalee, 12*

3 'I was so **excited** when I learned to ride a bike! I was very proud of myself because I was only four years old. At the time, my older brother had only just learned and he was already six!' ***Jaya, 13***

2 Find a maximum of seven key words and (short) phrases in each comment which show:

- what each child did
- why it was special
- how the experience made them feel.

Sumalee _____

Jaya _____

Callum _____

Cambridge Global English Stage 6 Activity Book Unit 1

3 Pronunciation

Listen to the noun form of the adjectives in bold in Activity 1. Choose the correct stress pattern.

1 terror   a ● ●   (b ● ●)
2 beauty   a ● ●   b ● ●
3 excitement a ● ● ● b ● ● ●
4 amazement a ● ● ●   b ● ● ●
5 satisfaction a ● ● ● ● b ● ● ● ●
6 bravery   a ● ● ●   b ● ● ●

4 Word study Adjective and noun forms

Complete the sentences with adjectives and nouns from Activities 1 and 3. Use a different word in each sentence.

1 When I finally passed that difficult Maths exam, I felt really ___satisfied___.
2 We always have a feeling of _____ before a long holiday.
3 What _____ flowers! There are so many colours!
4 My uncle has a fear of flying. The last time he travelled by plane, he was _____.
5 Fire fighters are _____ because they often risk their lives.

5 Use of English

Complete the sentences using the correct form of the verb.

1 She _has won_ three music competitions in two years. (win)
2 What is the nicest place you _____ ever _____? (see)
3 He _____ never _____ to another country. (go)
4 She _____ Japanese food. (not / try)

Use of English

Present perfect
We use the present perfect to talk about experiences in the past, but we don't say exactly when they happened. We form the tense with **has/have** + past participle.
Have you ever **seen** the sea?
I **haven't been** on a rollercoaster again.

6 Challenge
Write six sentences about things you have or haven't experienced.

I have tried Vietnamese food.

I haven't been to a very cold country.

3 Inspiring people

1 Word study Words connected to music
Complete the paragraph with words from the box.

The Recycled Orchestra are a group of teenage ¹ _musicians_ from South America that ² _____ famous pieces of music on special musical instruments made of recycled rubbish. These ³ _____ musicians don't need expensive instruments and record ⁴ _____ to create wonderful music. They have become well known in their country and abroad, where many people ⁵ _____ their talent and their resourceful approach to music. A documentary film has already been made about them. What next? A recording ⁶ _____ maybe …

~~musicians~~
producers
performs
contract
admire
talented

Recycled Orchestra

2 Listen to Gabi's presentation about the Recycled Orchestra. Circle the correct answer.

1 The Recycled Orchestra are from   a (Paraguay.)   b Panama.

2 Their instruments are made from rubbish from a site
   a in the capital city.   b near their own town.

3 The orchestra have played   a in their country and abroad.
   b only in their country.

4 The orchestra play   a only classical music.   b classical and rock music.

5 Gabi says she admires   a people who have clever ideas.
   b the person who made the orchestra's first instrument.

6 At the end of the presentation, Gabi   a plays some music.
   b shows a short part of a film.

3 Listen again and circle the correct sequencing phrases.

1 Today (**I'm going to**) / **First of all, I'll** talk about a group of people …
2 **First of all**, / **As well as this**, have a look at some pictures of …
3 **As I said**, / **Since then**, the orchestra play very unusual instruments …
4 **Since then**, / **As well as this**, the orchestra has performed …
5 **As well as this**, / **Since then**, they have appeared in a movie.
6 **To sum up**, / **To finish**, I chose to talk about the Recycled Orchestra because …

4 Challenge
Complete Kurt's presentation below with the correct sentences a–g.

a To sum up, I chose to talk about Tommy because
b As I said in my introduction, this presentation is about Tommy my cousin.
c since then, he has done two more parachute jumps
d Today I'm going to talk about my cousin Tommy
e As well as this, he does football practice with children
f To finish, I'm going to show you a little video that Tommy made
g First of all, I'm going to show you some pictures.

¹ _d_ who I really admire. ² ____ and I want you to tell me why you think I admire him so much. ³ ____ He's ten years older than me and he's studying Sports Science at university. Two years ago he did something amazing – he did a parachute jump for charity from a plane. He raised lots of money to help people who have bad injuries and need help to walk again. And ⁴ ____ and raised even more money! ⁵ ____ in his neighbourhood every Saturday morning. He doesn't get paid – he does it for free. This means that more kids can come to the football practice. ⁶ ____ he is a very kind and fun person who gives up his free time to help other people. I also think he is very brave to do a parachute jump. ⁷ ____ before he did the parachute jump …

Cambridge Global English **Stage 6 Activity Book Unit 1**

4 Extraordinary experiences

1 **Read** the biography of Fabrice Muamba. Put the paragraphs in order. Use the headings below to help you.

1 Who the biography is about and why he is well known.

2 His background and what happened before his success.

3 Examples of his success and achievements.

4 Up-to-date information about him.

a When Fabrice collapsed on the pitch, the doctors fought very hard to save his life. They succeeded, and football fans all over the country celebrated his recovery. Sadly, Fabrice has stopped playing football, but he says he is thankful that he is alive. He has thanked the doctors, who he says, 'never gave up on me'. ____

b This is the story of an extraordinary second chance. In March 2012, Fabrice Muamba, the British football hero, was playing for his team, Bolton Wanderers. While thousands of football fans were cheering in the stadium, thousands more were watching the game on TV. Then suddenly Fabrice collapsed on the pitch. The fans watched as doctors ran to help him. He had a heart attack and his heart stopped for over an hour. The game was stopped. Everybody thought that he was dead. _1_

c Fabrice couldn't speak English when he arrived in England, but several years later he got excellent exam results, especially in English, French and Mathematics. But he also had a great talent for football and he became a Premier League player in 2008. ____

d Fabrice was born in the Democratic Republic of Congo, Africa, in 1988. When he was 11 years old, his family had to leave their country because they were in danger. They came to the UK and Fabrice went to school in London. ____

2 Read the biography again in order and answer the questions.

1. Who is the biography about?
2. What happened to him in March 2012?
3. Where was he born?
4. How old was he when he came to Britain?
5. What success did he have at school?
6. When did he become a top club player?
7. Does Fabrice play football now?
8. Who did he say a special thank you to?

Use of English

Past continuous
We use the past continuous to describe past actions happening at the same time as another action.
While thousands of football fans **were cheering** in the stadium,

past

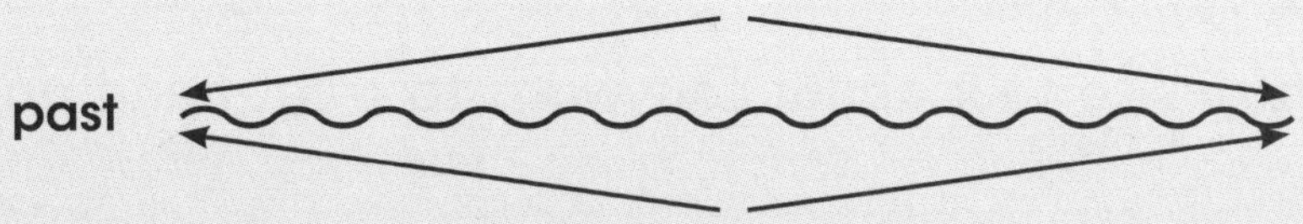

thousands more **were watching** the game on TV.

3 Use of English
Complete the sentences. Use the correct form of the past continuous with the verbs from the box.

study	learn
lie	work
~~play~~	~~cheer~~
celebrate	get
play	go

1. While Fabrice <u>was playing</u> football, the fans <u>were cheering</u> in the stadium.
2. While Fabrice _____ on the pitch, doctors _____ hard to save his life.
3. While he _____ hard at school, he _____ football for youth teams.
4. While he _____ English, he _____ to school in London.
5. While he _____ better in hospital, football fans _____ his recovery.

4  **Challenge**
Write a biography about a well-known person. Use the text on page 10 to help you.

5 An inspiring life

1 **Read** the biography of Helen Keller again and decide if these sentences are **T (true)** or **F (false)**. Correct the false sentences.

1 When Helen was born, it was easy for blind and deaf people to get a good education. _False. It was difficult because there were few opportunities._

2 Helen was seven years old when she lost her sight and hearing.

3 Helen's teacher taught her words by letting her touch objects as well as spell them.

4 Helen learned to speak when she was 20 years old.

5 Helen learned to read several other languages.

6 Helen studied at a very good university.

7 When she wrote her first book, people could only read it in English.

8 Helen visited a lot of countries to talk about fair ways to treat blind and deaf people.

| 12 | ~~100~~ | 7 | 10 | 18 | 30 | 20 | 39 |

2 Complete the sentences with a number from the box. Then put the sentences about Helen's life in the order they happened.

a When she was _____ , she went to university. _____

b Helen was born over _100_ years ago. _1_

c When she was _____ years old, her parents found her a good teacher. _____

d When she was _____ months old, she lost her sight and hearing. _____

e When she was _____ , Helen learned to speak. _____

f Helen visited _____ countries and met _____ US presidents. _____

g One day she learned _____ new words with her teacher. _____

12 Cambridge Global English Stage 6 Activity Book Unit 1

3 **Vocabulary** Achievements

Complete the sentences with a word from the box. Use the correct form of the verb.

> do research   raise money   write an article
> receive an award   ~~give a speech~~   go to university

1 Our head teacher usually _gives a speech_ at the end of term. She talks about all the good things that have happened during the term.

2 My cousin wants to _____ to study to be a doctor.

3 A man in our town _____ for bravery last year because he rescued someone from a fire.

4 We sold lots of things at the school fair and _____ for charity.

5 Last term, we _____ about sports day for our school newsletter.

6 Scientists are _____ all the time to try and find a cure for cancer.

4 **Challenge** Helping blind and deaf people

You can see these signs in public places all over the world. What do you think they mean? Where might you see them? Use the words in the box to help you.

You might see picture a in a library. It means there is help for deaf people.

a

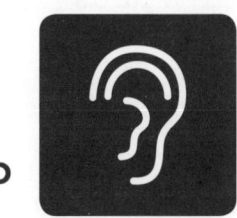
b

c

d

e

f Braille

> sign language
> guide dog
> blind
> deaf
> help
> support
> assistance
> allowed
> braille

Cambridge Global English Stage 6 Activity Book Unit 1

6 Unit 1 Revision

1 Multiple-choice quiz

1 At the weekends I really love meeting <u>up</u> with my friends.

   a on   (b up)   c in

2 My brother isn't really into sport. He prefers more creative activities like ___ .

   a playing football   b playing basketball   c taking photos

3 What ___ like doing in your free time?

   a you   b you do   c do you

4 Two years ago I flew in a helicopter. I remember the feeling of ___ so well!

   a excited   b exciting   c excitement

5 Have you ever ___ an elephant?

   a seen   b see   c saw

6 I ___ never tried Italian food.

   a have   b haven't   c has

7 I felt so nervous when I ___ my song in front of the whole school.

   a produced   b performed   c admired

8 will.i.am is a singer and songwriter; ___ this, he gives money to educational projects.

   a to sum up   b instead of   c as well as

9 Now why didn't I think ___ that idea?

   a of   b in   c on

10 While I was at your house yesterday, my sister was ___ basketball.

   a play   b played   c playing

11 Our class produced a calendar of pictures to ___ money for charity.

   a rise   b raise   c ride

12 Scientists have to ___ research to find cures for serious illnesses.

   a make   b put   c do

My global progress

Think about what you have studied in this unit. Answer the questions below.

1 What topics did you like and why?

2 What activities did you like and why?

3 What did you find challenging and why?

4 What help do you need now?

5 What would you like to find out more about?

6 What topics and activities relate to other subjects at your school?

2 School

1 My school day

1 Vocabulary School subjects
Complete the words and then complete the sentences below.

1 I_____ic _d___t__n   2 S c i e n c e   3 _r___ch
4 _a___o___l H_s____y   5 A__b_c   6 _p_n_s_
7 Ar_ and _e__gn   8 P_y_ _c_l Ed_c___i_n
9 S_c_al S__d__s

Subjects I study: _____

Subjects I haven't studied: _____

Subjects I like: _____

2 Read and compare school life in Egypt with your school day.

> Hi, I'm Omar and I live with my family in Alexandria, a big city in Egypt in North Africa. I'm twelve years old and I've just started 7th Grade. Here's how I spend a typical day at school.
>
> I leave my home at about 7.40am and get to school by 8am I live quite near to my school so I always walk. When I get to school, I usually play basketball for ten minutes until the bell rings. School starts at 8.15am, but first we do ten minutes of exercises to start the day – physical exercises like stretching. Then classes start at 8.25am There are nine classes a day, each lasting 45 minutes. We study Science, Maths, Social Studies and Computers, as well as Arabic, English and French. As well as these subjects, we also study Art and Music.
>
> I'm keen on Science because I love doing experiments and I like Maths too, because I enjoy solving problems with numbers. If I could choose, I'd like to have more Science lessons instead of Art. I'm not very good at Art!

Cambridge Global English Stage 6 Activity Book Unit 2

3 Read the text again and complete the table about you and Omar.

	Omar	Me
1 Travel to school	walks	
2 Before classes start		
3 Time classes start		
4 Length of classes		
5 School subjects		
6 Subjects we like		

4 **Use of English** Linking phrases
Complete the next part of Omar's text with **as well as** and **instead of**.

My cousin goes to a school in the next town. We are the same age and in 7th Grade, but we are quite different at school. He studies German, ¹ _instead of_ French.
² _____ Studies and Maths, he's really into Art and Music. He wishes that there were more Art classes ³ _____ Science! He's good at painting, ⁴ _____ photography. And he's quite good at languages. He speaks English, ⁵ _____ Arabic.

Use of English

Linking phrases instead of / as well as + noun

We use **as well as** to express something that is done **in addition** to something else.
As well as these subjects, we also study art and music.
We use **instead of** when something **replaces** something else.
I'd like to have more science lessons **instead of** art.

5 **Challenge**
Compare your school day to Omar's. Use your notes and the linking phrases from Activity 3 to make sentences.

At my school we study Spanish instead of Arabic.

As well as 45-minute lessons, we have classes for one hour.

_____

_____

_____

Cambridge Global English Stage 6 Activity Book Unit 2   17

2 What is brain power?

Reading strategy Finding specific information
Tick the strategy which will help you to scan a text. Use the strategy before you read the text below.
- Look at any pictures ☐
- Decide what information you want to find first. ☐
- Look up specific words in the dictionary. ☐

1 Read
Look at the study tips, a–d. Then complete the children's comments about study habits with one of the tips.

a use a Mind Map	b be relaxed
c use visual images	d teach someone else

1 I think you have to _____ to study well. Unless you're calm, you won't be able to study properly. If I'm worried about something, I can't concentrate, so I talk about the problem with someone I can trust – then I feel better.

2 When I'm studying, I _____ to help me remember information. It really helps. When I'm trying to remember an important fact, I think of a picture to go with it, or connect it with a photograph or chart in my text book.

3 When I'm trying to remember information for an exam, I find it really helps to _____ first. So I explain it to one of my friends or someone in my family. If I can explain it to someone else, I'm sure I'll remember it later in the exam.

4 When I have to remember something for an exam, I _____ or spidergram to make notes. You write the topic in the middle of the page, and add ideas and information using lines – so it looks like a spider! For me this is the best way to make notes. If you don't make good notes first, you won't remember things so well in the exam.

2 📝 Which study habits in Activity 1 do you do? Which do you think is the best advice? Why?

3 Use of English
Read the *Use of English* box. Choose the correct word to complete the sentences.

1 If you **use** / **will use** pictures, you'll remember things better.
2 If you are worried about something, you **won't** / **don't** concentrate well.
3 You won't remember important information, unless you **make** / **will make** good notes.
4 If you feel relaxed, you **would** / **will** study better.
5 Unless you **will find** / **find** a quiet place to work, you won't study well.
6 If you **can** / **could** teach the information to someone else, you will remember it better.

> **Use of English**
>
> **1st conditional with if/unless**
>
> We use the 1st conditional to express future events that are likely to happen. We form the structure with **if/unless** + present simple + **will/won't** + verb
> **Unless** you're calm, you **won't** be able to study properly.
> (In this sentence, **unless** means 'if you're not ...')
> **If I can** explain it to someone else, I'm sure **I'll** remember it later in the exam.
> **If** you don't make good notes first, you **won't** remember things so well in the exam.

4 📝 **Challenge**
Use the pictures and prompts to write more advice about good study habits. Make two sentences for each picture using **if** and **unless**.

1 sleep / study
2 drink water / concentrate
3 do exercise / remember
4 eat healthy food / energy

If you sleep well, you'll study better.
Unless you sleep well you won't study better.

3 A problem shared

1 Vocabulary Behaviour

Complete the dialogue with a word from the box in the correct form.

> tell us off   ~~mess about~~   bully   join in with   laugh at

A: I don't like my project group. Everyone ¹ _messes about_ and wastes time. I'm the only one who does any work.

B: Why don't you talk to them? Tell them how you feel.

A: I've done that, but they just ² _____ me. They think it's all a big joke. The teacher always ³ _____ because he thinks we don't do any work.

B: Oh no! Why don't you tell the teacher what's happening?

A: Because if I do that, they might ⁴ _____ me. They're all bigger than me!

B: I know! Come and ⁵ _____ my group. We need another team member.

2 Read about the school problems. What problem does each child have?

1 I am feeling really nervous about starting a new school in September. My family is going to move to a new town and I will start my new school in Year 6. I'm frightened because I won't know anyone. Can you give me some advice about making new friends?

Dana, 10

2 I got a really bad result in my maths test last week. It is an important test and I'm not very good at Maths. My mum keeps asking me about the result and I'm too scared to tell her. If I don't tell her soon, my teacher will email her. What should I do?

Max, 11

3 Word study Giving advice and suggestions

Complete the answers (1–5) with a phrase (a–e). Then match the answers with the problems in Activity 2.

a Why don't you ask … .
b I think you should visit … .
c … you could think … .
d How about joining … .
e If I were you I would be brave … .

1 Before you tell your mum, _c_ of some ways to improve your Maths grades in the future – then she will know you are trying hard and she probably won't be so angry.

(Problem __)

2 ___ if some children in your new class can show you around the school? Then you will already know them when you join the class.

(Problem __)

3 ___ and tell your mum about the result. If you don't tell her yourself, she'll be more angry when she hears the result from the teacher.

(Problem __)

4 If you think in a positive way, then you'll feel better. This is an adventure and the chance to meet new friends! ___ your new school before you start.

(Problem __)

4 Challenge

Read Ismail's problem and write four possible solutions.

> In a few weeks' time I have an important exam. It tests most of the subjects I am studying at the moment. I feel very nervous and I'm sure I'm going to fail! Can you give me some advice about preparing for the exam and feeling less nervous?
>
> Ismail, 11

I think you should … .

Why don't you … ?

Cambridge Global English Stage 6 Activity Book Unit 2   21

4 Starting something new

1 Vocabulary Extra-curricular activities
Circle the noun phrases in the text for extra-curricular activities in the school brochure.

At Park Elementary School, we offer a wide range of extra-curricular activities that help your child practise their talents and interests. Over 40% of Year 6 students go to our popular (computer club), which meets once a week. We also offer Art, Music and Drama groups and a chess club, that all meet twice a month. Young chefs can join a monthly cookery group, to learn about food from different countries and young journalists can write for the school newsletter. Let's also not forget our prize-winning school choir, who practise once a week.

We are proud to say that about 80% of Year 6 students belong to an after-school club. This pie chart shows after-school activities for one Year 6 class.

Park Elementary School - Extra-curricular activities

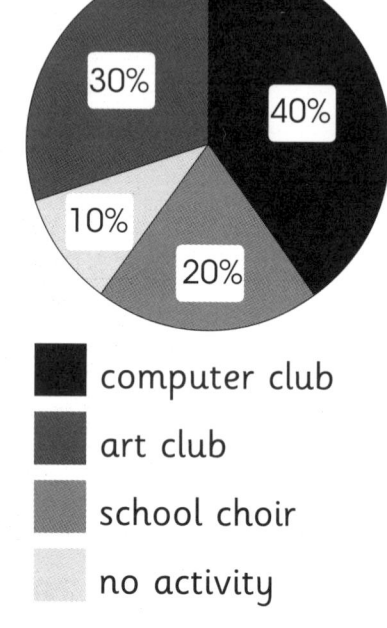

2 Read the pie chart in the text above. There are 30 students in the class. How many students take part in each activity? How many don't do an activity?

3 Recording information

Look at the pie chart below and read the notes about extra-curricular activities in other classes. Change the number of students into percentages.

Extra-curricular activities: 60 students

- Computer club: 21 students   _____
- Drama club: 15 students   _____
- Art club: 9 students   _____
- School choir: 6 students   _10%_
- No activity: 6 students   _____
- Chess club: 3 students   _____

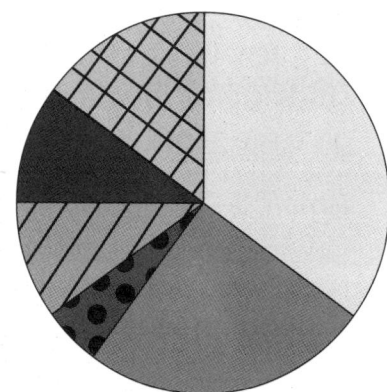

Extra-curricular activities: 60 students

22 Cambridge Global English **Stage 6 Activity Book Unit 2**

4 **Read** the email below to the head teacher, Mr Osman, and match with a topic.

Start an activity group   Buy new equipment   Organise an event

5 **Use of English**
Complete with modal verbs from the box.

could   should   would

Dear Mr Osman

We ¹ _would_ like to ask your permission to organise a talent show for the end of term. There are some very talented students in Year 6 and we think it would be a good opportunity to show their skills to the school.

We ² _____ like to have six acts in our final show. Lots of our classmates want to take part, so we ³ _____ like to have auditions to choose the final six. We ⁴ _____ also like to have four judges and we ⁵ _____ like you to be one of them. Everyone agrees that you ⁶ _____ be a judge, as well as three other teachers.

If you agree to our idea, ⁷ _____ we hold the auditions in the music room on Wednesdays after school? Mrs Aziz, the music teacher, says this is OK with her, but we ⁸ _____ ask your permission first.

If you like our idea, ⁹ _____ we come and see you to tell you more?

Yours sincerely,

Nahlia Roy and Lisa Malik

---

6 Use **would**, **could** and **should** to write sentences.

1 Ask for permission to start an Art club.

2 Ask your art teacher politely if he/she will help you to organise the club.

3 Give some advice about preparations needed before the Art club can start.

 7 **Challenge**

Write an email to your head teacher asking for permission to start an Art club. Use Activities 5 and 6 to help you.

Cambridge Global English **Stage 6 Activity Book Unit 2**   23

5 Classroom politics

1 **Read** the extract again in your Learner's Book on page 28. Put the sentences in the summary in the correct order of the story.

  a Jeff sits down and smiles at Bradley. Bradley looks the other way. _____

  b At the beginning, Bradley Chalkers is sitting alone at his desk in class. None of the other children want to sit next to him and the teacher doesn't like him. He doesn't want to be friendly to them either. __1__

  c The bell rings for break time. Bradley goes out of the classroom alone. Jeff calls him and tries to be friendly. Bradley is surprised. _____

  d Mrs Ebbel begins the lesson. Bradley doesn't want to listen. _____

  e Bradley is unfriendly to Jeff and threatens him. He ask for a dollar. _____

  f Mrs Ebbel, asks Jeff to sit next to Bradley, because it is the only empty seat in the classroom. She is sorry that Jeff has to sit next to Bradley. _____

  g Bradley shows his language test to the class; then he cuts it up with _____

  h Mrs Ebbel, introduces a new boy, Jeff Fishkin, to the class. _____

  i Mrs Ebbel returns a language test to the class. She points out that everyone in the class got a good mark, except Bradley who failed the test. _____

2 Choose the answer that best describes some of the ideas in the story.

  1 Jeff is friendly towards Bradley because **he hasn't got any opinion about him**. / **the teacher told him to be friendly**.

  2 When Jeff smiles at him, Bradley looks the other way because **he wants to look out of the window**. / **he doesn't know what to do**.

  3 At break time, Bradley is **very surprised**/ **very happy** when Jeff tries to make friends with him.

3 **Vocabulary** Body language
Complete the sentences with a word from the box. Use the correct form of the verb.

| hurry   scribble   stare   ~~shrug~~   shake |

1 She <u>shrugged</u> her shoulders because she didn't know what the answer was.
2 He _____ the answers so quickly that the teacher couldn't understand anything he had written.
3 She _____ at the boy in amazement. She couldn't believe what he had just done.
4 'No, that's not true, I didn't say that,' she said as she _____ her head.
5 He _____ to class because he thought he was going to be late.

63 4 **Pronunciation** Silent letters
Listen and repeat the words from the story. Which letters are silent?

1 wou<u>l</u>d   2 which   3 right   4 turned   5 stared

5 **Values** Treating classmates fairly
Choose and circle the best word to describe what you think happens in your class.

1 **All** / **most** / **some** / **a few** of us work well together in teams.
2 **All** / **most** / **some** / **a few** of us help each other if someone doesn't understand something.
3 **All** / **most** / **some** / **a few** of us are nice to each other, even if we are not close friends.
4 **All** / **most** / **some** / **a few** of us share equipment without arguments.
5 **All** / **most** / **some** / **a few** of us get a fair chance to show what we can do.
6 **All** / **most** / **some** / **a few** of us are quiet when someone is answering the teacher's question.

6 Unit 2 Revision

1 Vocabulary
Match the sentence halves.

1 If you don't hurry,   a Science and National History.
2 Last term I belonged to   b come and join in with us!
3 The subjects I'm really into are   c she can join the school choir.
4 It's unkind   d the computer club.
5 Don't work on your own –   e to laugh at other people's mistakes.
6 If she can sing well   f you'll be late for school.

2 Use of English
Circle the correct word to complete the email.

Dear Head teacher

Our class [1] **could / would** like to ask your permission to buy a new laptop for our classroom. We have raised $300 from our stall at the school fair, [2] **as well as / instead of** $100 from selling cakes in break time last week – so we have a total of $400. Our class teacher says that we [3] **should / would** spend the money on something we can all use. [4] **Unless / If** we buy a laptop, it will help us with our project work because we [5] **will / won't** be able to use the Internet in our classroom. Please [6] **should / could** you let us know if you like our idea?

Yours faithfully, Class 6B

3 Over to you
Complete the sentences with your own ideas.

1 Instead of _____ , I would like to study _____ .

2 At school, I'm good at _____ as well as _____ .

3 If you can't do your homework, you should _____ .

4 I would like to ask my class teacher _____ .

5 Unless you eat healthy food, _____

6 If you don't listen in class, _____ .

Cambridge Global English Stage 6 Activity Book Unit 2

My global progress

Think about what you have studied in this unit. Answer the questions below.

1 What topics did you like and why?
_____
_____

2 What activities did you like and why?
_____
_____

3 What did you find challenging and why?
_____
_____

4 What help do you need now?
_____
_____

5 What would you like to find out more about?
_____
_____

6 What topics and activities relate to other subjects at your school?
_____
_____

3 Sport

1 Get active

1 Vocabulary Sports
Find ten types of sport in the word search and write about them below.

Sports I've tried

_____

Sports I often do

_____

Popular sports in my country

_____

F	H	O	C	K	E	Y	V	H	S	L	B
G	O	E	G	P	A	K	H	B	L	J	A
Q	V	O	L	L	E	Y	B	A	L	L	S
S	A	Z	T	P	V	I	S	D	J	T	K
W	I	T	Q	B	J	M	E	M	B	E	E
I	J	G	H	Q	A	B	K	I	T	N	T
M	U	H	J	L	H	L	H	N	G	N	B
M	D	I	A	B	E	T	L	T	B	I	A
I	O	J	V	L	A	T	S	O	M	S	L
N	H	J	Y	R	Y	A	I	N	G	I	L
G	Y	M	N	A	S	T	I	C	S	V	Q
J	Z	P	I	Z	Q	G	V	P	S	I	S

2 Vocabulary Equipment
Complete the sentences with a word from the box.

shin pads   racquet   ~~goggles~~   shuttlecock   goalposts   trunks

1 You wear _____goggles_____ to protect your eyes when you are swimming.

2 You wear _____ to protect the front part of your legs between your knees and ankles.

3 You hit a _____ when you are playing badminton.

4 Boys wear _____ or shorts when they go swimming.

5 You hit the ball with a _____ when you are playing tennis or badminton.

6 _____ tell you where the goal is when you are playing football.

Incidental artwork from LB

3 Read

Which sport in Activity 1 are the comments about? _____

1. You can play this sport on the beach, on grass or on a court in a sports centre. The only equipment you need is a net and a ball, and shorts and a T-shirt or vest to play in.

2. Each team has six players and the rules are more complicated than you think! Players must stop the ball from touching the ground in their team's side of the net.

3. You hit the ball with your hands, but you can't throw or catch the ball and you're not allowed to touch the net. You must have strong legs and lots of stamina because there is a lot of jumping and diving in the game.

4 Match a topic to a comment.

Basic rules _____   Parts of the body used _____

Location and equipment _____

5 Write a paragraph about a sport that you do or know something about. Use Activities 2, 3 and 4 to help you.

6 Challenge Interpreting information

Read Zainab's survey notes. Complete the bar chart with the information. Answer the questions below.

Survey: 30 students

Swimming: 15 students

Basketball: 2 students

Badminton: 3 students

Football: 10 students

What is your favourite sport?

(Number of students / Favourite sports)

1 Which is the most popular sport in the class?

2 Which sport do a third of the class like best?

3 Which sports do a few of the classmates like?

2 Yes I can

Strategy check! Scanning
Tick the strategy which will help you to scan a text. Use the strategy before you read the text below.

- Look at pictures. ☐
- Read the whole text in detail. ☐
- Read the text quickly for the main points. ☐

The Paralympic Games

The Paralympic Games is one of the largest international sports events in the world. It takes place every two years alongside the summer and winter Olympic Games. These elite sportsmen and women are the best at their sport, despite the fact that every one of them has a disability.

It started when a German doctor organised a sports competition for 2nd World War soldiers at the 1948 London Olympic Games. These soldiers had injuries to their spines, but they were excellent wheelchair athletes. The doctor wanted to show their talents alongside the skills of the Olympic athletes. The Paralympic Games grew from this competition.

Today, in the 21st century Paralympic Games, there are thousands of world-class athletes from nearly 150 different countries. Paralympians compete on the track in wheelchair racing and on blades; in swimming and rowing events in the water; in wheelchair basketball and rugby on a court; skiing on mountain slopes and cycling in the velodrome. There are many more events too. The focus of the Games is always on what the athletes can achieve and never on their disabilities.

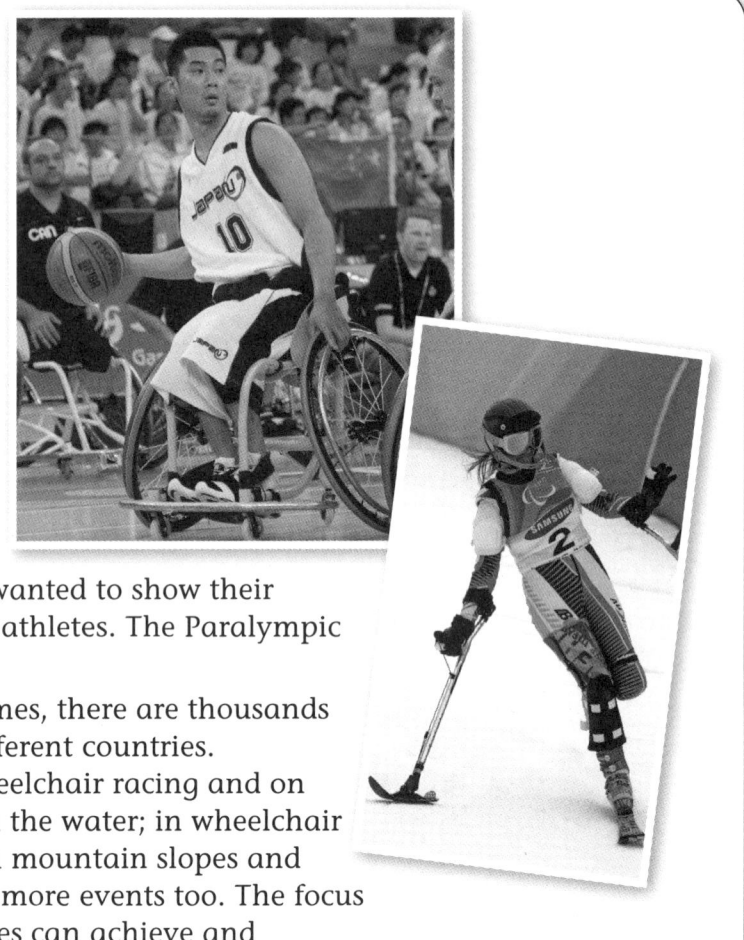

1 **Read** the text and answer the questions in your notebook.

1 What is the Paralympic Games?
2 What do Paralympic athletes have in common?
3 How many countries compete in the Paralympic Games today?
4 Find five types of sports that you can see at the Paralympic Games.

Use of English

Reported speech in the present
Direct statement
'I think about what I can do, not what I can't do.'
Reported statement
Jonnie says (that) he thinks about what he can do, not what he can't.
Reported Wh- questions
Direct question
'What is your attitude to your sport?'
Reported question
He wants to know what his attitude to his sport is.

2 Use of English
Read the *Use of English* box and the mini-interview with Paralympic athlete, Jonnie Peacock. Report the interviewer's questions and Jonnie's replies.

Interviewer: What is your attitude to your sport?

Jonnie: I think about what I can do, not what I can't do.

Interviewer: What is your record time for running the 100 metres?

Jonnie: It's 10.9 seconds, at the 2012 London Paralympics.

Interviewer: What is your target now?

Jonnie: My goal now is to run the 100 metres in 10.6 seconds!

1 <u>He wants to know what his attitude his sport is.</u>
2 <u>Jonnie says (that) he thinks about what he can do, not what he can't.</u>
3 _____
4 _____
5 _____
6 _____

3 Challenge

Write questions to ask your favourite sports star. Write his/her answers in reported questions and statements.

Cambridge Global English Stage 6 Activity Book Unit 3   31

3 Giving instructions

1 Vocabulary Parts of the body
Complete the words to describe parts of the body. Answer the questions.

h i p   t _ _ g _ _   _ h _ _ l _ e _   _ _ _ rt

h _ _ s _ _ _ _ g _   _ o t _ _   a _ k _ _ e s   k _ _ _ s

1 Which parts are connected to your legs and feet? _Thighs,_____
2 Which are connected to your arms? _____
3 Which part pumps the blood around your body? _____

64 2 Listen and put the pictures in order for the Warrior pose.

64 3 Listen again and follow the instructions. Which parts of your body did you use in this exercise? Which muscles worked the hardest?

_____

32 Cambridge Global English Stage 6 Activity Book Unit 3

4 **Use of English**
Correct the sentences by replacing the underlined verb with another verb from the box.

> **Use of English**
>
> **need/should/mustn't for advice and instructions**
>
> We use **need** when something is necessary.
> First we **need to** get your heart pumping …
> We use **should** to give advice.
> You **should** warm up your hips too.
> We use **mustn't** when something is not allowed.
> You **mustn't** start running without warming up your leg muscles.

| mustn't   need   should |

1 You ~~should~~ _mustn't_ do any hard exercise without warming up first.
2 When you warm up, you <u>need</u> _____ stretch your muscles too.
3 You <u>mustn't</u> _____ to drink water while you are running.
4 You <u>should</u> _____ force your muscles when you stretch them or you might hurt yourself.
5 People of all ages <u>should</u> _____ to do some regular exercise.
6 Everyone <u>needs</u> _____ try to do some exercise every day to stay healthy.

5 **Use of English** Circle the correct verb to complete the text.

Where does yoga come from?

Yoga is a type of exercise that originated in India and is thousands of years old. You [1] **mustn't /(should)** try yoga if you want a strong and flexible body, as well as a relaxed mind. There are millions of people from all over the world who agree! But first, there are some facts you [2] **need / should** know.

Yoga is great for kids of all ages, but you [3] **mustn't / need** try difficult yoga exercises without an instructor. Some yoga exercises look easier than they are; the instructor [4] **needs / should** to make sure you are doing them in the correct way or you might hurt yourself. You [5] **should / mustn't** do yoga without warming up first and you [6] **should / mustn't** wear loose, comfortable clothes. You [7] **need / should** to have enough space around you to stretch your arms and legs. When you are doing the yoga exercises, you [8] **mustn't / need to** take long breaths in and out – if you do this, you'll feel energetic and relaxed at the same time! Want to try a yoga exercise? Try the Warrior pose in Activity 3!

4 Marathon achievement

1 **Read** the article. How much money has Millie's school raised for charity?

¹ <u>Every year in June</u>, our school does a Fun Run for charity ² <u>in our local park</u>. ³ <u>Hundreds of us go down to the park and run circuits around the lake and through the woods</u>. And even more people come down to the park to watch us and cheer us on.

And it's not just ⁴ <u>pupils who take part. There are teachers, parents, grandparents, aunts and uncles too – and even some dogs!</u> Some of us put on our running clothes, but a lot of us dress up in fancy dress costumes for the occasion. Last year there were superheroes and big furry animals doing the Fun Run too!

So far our school Fun Run has ⁵ <u>raised over $20 000 for charity</u>. We ask our family and friends to sponsor us for each circuit we run around the lake. The more circuits we do, the more money we raise for our favourite charities. We ⁶ <u>get fit</u> and charities benefit – so everyone's a winner!

School Magazine 3

2 ✏️ **Write** Make notes and write a summary

Read the article again. Match the underlined sentences with these headings.

a Where the Fun Run happens _____

b When it happens ___1___

c Reasons for taking part. _____

d What it is _____

e Who takes part _____

3 Match the sentences from the article with a word in the box with a similar meaning.

1 ... superheroes and big furry animals _costumes_

2 ... around the lake and through the woods

3 ... and even some dogs!

4 ... parents, grandparents, aunts and uncles ...

> pets
> ~~costumes~~
> families
> the park

⭐ **4 Challenge**

Use your notes to write a summary of Millie's article in 65–75 words.

_____
_____
_____
_____
_____
_____

5 🔢 **Calculations** Do the calculations and answer the questions.

1 Last year 1500 people watched the Fun Run in the park. This year there were twice as many. How many spectators were at the Fun Run this year?

_____

2 In the Fun Run last year, Millie ran 20 circuits around the lake in the park. Her family sponsored her $1.50 per circuit. How much money did she raise for charity?

_____

Cambridge Global English Stage 6 Activity Book Unit 3

5 Football crazy

1 **Read** the extract again from *Off side* by Tom Palmer. Decide if the sentences are **T (true)** or **F (false)**. Correct the false sentences in your notebook.

1 Danny and his dad go to every game their football team plays at home. _T_

2 Danny's dad is deaf. __

3 In the story, Danny and his dad are watching a match between the teams, City and United. __

4 During the match, Danny describes what's happening to his dad. __

5 The star City players, Anthony Owusu and Sam Roberts are defenders. __

6 During the match, Sam Roberts scores a goal. __

7 When the goal happens, the United fans cheer very loudly. __

8 After the goal, Danny explains to his dad what has happened. __

2 **Over to you**
Think about the story and answer the questions.

1 Did you like the story? What did / didn't you like about it?
_____
_____

2 Did you understand the story better by listening to it, as well as reading it? How does listening make a difference?
_____
_____

Read Descriptive words
When writers write a description, they often use words in a different way to the meaning in the dictionary. To help you understand a descriptive word, 1) think of the **theme** or **context** of the whole story; 2) look at **other words** and **sentences** in the section to help you guess its meaning.

3 **Vocabulary** Descriptive words
Find the words in the story and match to a definition.
Use the Reading strategy to help you.

a extremely good __
b bounced __
c a kick before the ball hits the ground __
d shocked, unable to move __
e a fast player in the middle of the field __
f two strong football players __

4 **Vocabulary** Different parts of a team
Match the words in the box to a description.

| midfield   defenders   (goal) keeper   strikers |

1 Players in the goal area who try to stop the other team from scoring.
2 The group of players that connect the defenders and strikers.
3 The main role of these players is to score goals.
4 A player who defends the goal in the area between the goal posts.

5 **Values** Team work
Write about any school 'team' that you belong to (e.g. a sports team, a project team, being part of a class). Describe the duties that you and the other team or class members have.

_____
_____
_____

Cambridge Global English Stage 6 Activity Book Unit 3   37

6 Unit 3: Revision

1 Crossword

Solve the puzzle with the missing words.

Down ↓

1 You should wear goggles if you go ____ .

2 The part of your leg between your ankle and thigh is your ____ .

4 You can play football ____ in a gym or outside on a pitch.

6 Hannah Cockroft won two gold ____ at the 2012 Paralympics.

7 This word means 'a strong hard hit'.

Across →

3 You mustn't start exercising without doing ____ up exercises.

5 You ____ a racquet and a shuttlecock to play badminton.

6 Your ____ need to be warm to work properly when you do sport.

8 A great thing about playing a sport is working together in a ____ .

9 My cousins ____ judo every Thursday evening.

10 In hockey, you need a ____ to hit the ball.

11 The objective in football, basketball and hockey is to score a ____ .

12 A big city marathon is often a ____ of 42 kilometres.

My global progress

Think about what you have studied in this unit. Answer the questions below.

1 What topics did you like and why?
_____
_____

2 What activities did you like and why?
_____
_____

3 What did you find challenging and why?
_____
_____

4 What help do you need now?
_____
_____

5 What would you like to find out more about?
_____
_____

6 What topics and activities relate to other subjects at your school?
_____
_____

4 The big screen

1 Describing films

1 **Vocabulary** Types of film
Complete the descriptions with a word from the box.

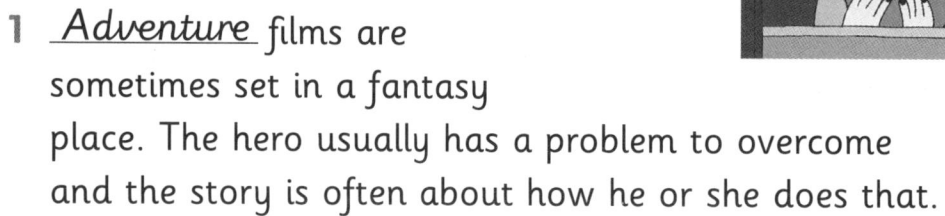

1 _Adventure_ films are sometimes set in a fantasy place. The hero usually has a problem to overcome and the story is often about how he or she does that.

2 _____ movies are set in the past and tell stories from 100 years ago or more.

3 _____ films are supposed to make you feel really scared.

4 _____ movies are set in the future. They imagine what life might be like 50 years or more from now. The setting is often space or another planet.

5 In _____ films, there is usually a hero in dangerous and exciting situations. These films are fast-moving and often very noisy!

6 _____ films make you laugh a lot and are not very serious.

7 _____ films are usually about serious situations in life. They are often sad and might make you cry in some parts!

8 Nowadays _____ films have fantastic special effects. This means that talented artists can create characters and scenery that comes to life on the movie screen.

> animation
> comedy
> ~~adventure~~
> science-fiction
> horror
> drama
> action
> historical

2 **Write**

What was the last film you saw? What type of film was it?
Which types of films do you like best? Which ones don't you enjoy?

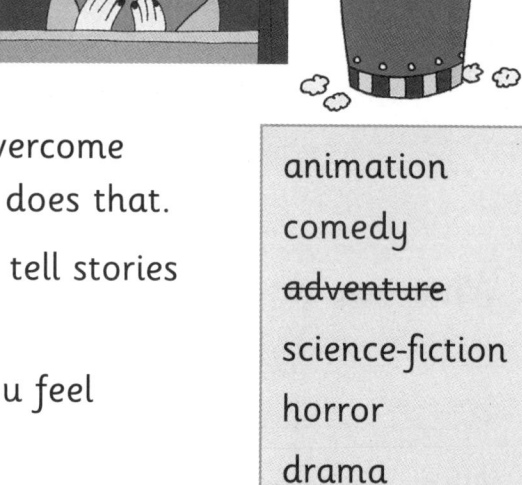

3 Vocabulary Strong adjectives

Find seven adjective pairs in the word snake and put them in the correct column.

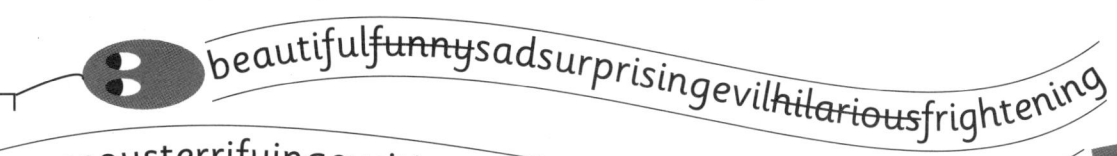

beautiful funny sad surprising evil hilarious frightening gorgeous terrifying exciting heartbreaking bad thrilling amazing

Adjectives	Strong adjectives
funny	hilarious

4 Use of English

Complete the sentences with the correct adverb from the *Use of English* box.

1 The special effects in the film were ~~a bit~~ / **really** gorgeous.

2 The animation was **absolutely** / **very** funny.

3 It was a **very** / **absolutely** bad movie and a waste of money.

4 It's **quite** / **absolutely** sad in some parts — we all cried!

5 I thought the story was **very** / **absolutely** terrifying; afterwards I couldn't sleep!

6 Watch the movie just for the scenery — it's **really** / **very** amazing!

> **Use of English**
>
> **Adverbs absolutely / really**
>
> We use **absolutely** and **really** and **not very** with strong adjectives.
>
> The film was ~~very~~ **absolutely hilarious**.
>
> We can use **really**, **very**, **quite** and **a bit** with other adjectives.
>
> It was **quite** slow in some parts and **a bit** boring.

5 Challenge

Choose adverbs and adjectives to describe your opinion of the images in the pictures.

a *I think that kitten is absolutely gorgeous! (It's so small and cute!)*

a   b   c   d

2 The first movies

> **Strategy check!** Listen for specific information
> Tick the strategy which will help you to listen for specific information. Use the strategy before you listen.
> - Listen to the recording but don't read the text first. ☐
> - Read the information first and make guesses about years or dates. ☐
> - When you listen again recheck the dates. ☐

65 1 Listen A brief history of animation
Listen and match the information with the years.

1 1900s _____
2 1928   _____
3 1937   _____
4 1940s – 1950s _____
5 1990s _____
6 1995   _____
7 2001   _a_

a *Shrek* becomes the first film to win an Academy Award for Best Animated Feature.

b The first animation films were made.

c *Toy Story* was released – the first full-length film animated on computers.

d *Snow White and the Seven Dwarves*, the first full-length animation film was produced by Walt Disney.

e Disney films became popular and were watched by millions of people in cinemas.

f Sound was added to cartoons for the first time. Mickey Mouse was also born!

g Computers were used for the first time to make animation films.

2 Pronunciation Saying decades
What does **the 1940s** mean?

a 1940   b 1940–1949

66 3 Listen
Listen and write the decade you hear. Then listen again and repeat.

a _____   b _____   c _____   d _____

Cambridge Global English **Stage 6 Activity Book Unit 4**

67 **4 Pronunciation** Saying years after 2000
Listen and write the correct year. Listen again and repeat.

1 a _2001_   b _____   c _____
2 a _____   b _____   c _____

5 Use of English Past simple passive

Correct the errors in these sentences. Use the *Use of English* box to help you.

1 The first film starring Mickey Mouse <u>was make</u> in the 1920s.

The first film starring Mickey Mouse was made in the 1920s.

2 The *Madagascar* films <u>was shown</u> in cinemas all over the world.

3 The first full-length animation film <u>were called</u> *Snow White and the Seven Dwarves*.

4 Computers <u>weren't use</u> to make animation films in the 1940s.

5 When <u>was the first cartoon create</u>?

Use of English

Past simple passive

We use this passive form to talk about events in the past. We want to focus on the event, not the person who did it.

The first animation films **were made** in the early 1900s.

Where **were** the first animation films **made**?

If we want to mention the person who did the action, we use **by**.

The first film starring Mickey Mouse **was produced by** Walt Disney.

6 Complete the sentences using the past simple passive.

1 Lots of Disney films __were produced__ (produce) in the 1960s and 70s.
2 The first *Toy Story* film _____ (create) in the 1990s.
3 The first animation films _____ (not make) in colour.
4 In the first cartoons, hundreds of drawings _____ (need) to produce just one minute of animation.
5 The award-winning animation film, *Shrek*, _____ (release) in 2001.

7 Challenge

Write a short paragraph about your favourite animation film.

_____ was released in 20 _____ . The main character is ... .

3 What makes a good film?

1 **Read** the answers below and match them to the questions.

> 1 Have you seen any good films recently?
> 2 What kind of film is it?
> 3 What's it about?
> 4 Where's it set?
> 5 Would you recommend it?

a It's set in India and a lot of the action takes place in the middle of the ocean.

b Yes, I saw *Life of Pi* at the cinema two weeks ago with my dad. It was amazing! __1__

c Yes, I would. I liked the scenes <u>where the boy faces the tiger</u>, and then makes friends with him. My dad didn't like the film though! He says he prefers films that have more realistic plots! But I thought the plot was interesting and exciting.

d It's an adventure movie which looks fantastic. There are some amazing scenes, with great special effects.

e It's about a boy called Pi who has an incredible adventure at sea. It starts in India where his family own a zoo. But they have to sell the zoo and all the animals. They decide to sail to Canada where they can sell the animals and build a new life. But on the way they have an accident and only Pi and a few animals survive. So Pi is left in the middle of the sea in a lifeboat with the wild animals. And one of them is a huge hungry tiger! The film is about how Pi survives … .

2 Read the answers again and answer the questions.

1 Which answer tells you about the **plot**? _____
2 Where is the **setting** for the film? _____
3 Which main **characters** are mentioned? _____

Cambridge Global English **Stage 6 Activity Book Unit 4**

3 Use of English
Read the *Use of English* box. Underline five relative clauses in the answers in Activity 1 (one has been done for you).

4 Choose the correct relative pronoun to complete the sentences.

1 I like the ending **that** / **(when)** / **who** the hero finally saves the planet.

2 My little sister doesn't like movies **that** / **who** / **where** are too long.

3 The most exciting scenes are **who** / **that** / **where** the superheroes are flying between buildings.

4 The special effects are so good **that** / **where** / **who** you think they are real.

5 The best scene is **that** / **when** / **who** the heroes finally discover the secret palace.

6 It's about a girl **where** / **who** / **when** discovers a lost city.

7 Is that the scene **that** / **who** / **where** the dinosaurs escape into the city?

8 He is a character **where** / **when** / **who** always does the right thing.

Use of English

Relative clauses

Relative clauses are parts of a sentence that start with a relative pronoun.

The characters are so life-like **that** they look like real people.

It's about a group of superheroes, **who** have amazing abilities

There is a good scene **where** one of the heroes goes to Antarctica.

I liked the ending **when** the superheroes win.

5 Challenge
Use relative clauses to complete the sentences about the film, *Epic*.

1 *Epic* is an adventure story ___that___ looks amazing.

2 It's about a young girl _____ goes on a special journey.

3 She is transported to a forest _____ there is a fight between good and evil.

4 There are a group of villains _____ want to destroy the forest.

5 One of the nicest scenes is _____ she meets the other characters for the first time.

6 It is a film _____ I would recommend to my friends.

Cambridge Global English Stage 6 Activity Book Unit 4

4 Creating film scenes

1 Vocabulary Reporting verbs
Complete the dialogues with a verb from the box.

> sniggered ~~whispered~~ sighed asked insisted

1 'Shh! Don't speak so loudly! They'll hear you!' she _whispered_.

2 'I won't take no for an answer! You have to come with us!' he _____.

3 'It's so funny! He still doesn't realise that he's put up his tent on an ants' nest!' he _____.

4 'What time is it?' she _____ for the third time.

5 'Oh no, you've done it again! I'm tired of it! Don't you ever learn?' _____ Dad.

2 Read the storyboard and put the pictures in the correct order.

The Light in the Garden

1 It was already past midnight and Lily couldn't sleep. She didn't know why. Then she realised that her sister, Lara, was awake too … .

2 Lily got up to close the curtain. It seemed unusually bright outside for a cloudy winter night. Then she noticed the light in the corner of the garden.

3 Lara got out of bed and joined Lily at the window. The two girls looked at the light in amazement. Lara wanted to go outside and look at it close up.

4 Lily looked at her sister in shock. She didn't want to go out in the cold dark garden in the middle of the night. But her sister had other ideas!

a ____   b ____   c ____   d _1_

3 **Punctuation** Direct speech

Add speech marks, exclamation marks and commas to the dialogue. Then match the dialogue with the pictures and text in Activity 1.

1 'You are joking!' exclaimed Lily, 'I'm not going out there at this time of night!'

'Well, I'll go on my own then, replied Lara, 'I want to find out what it is.'

Picture __b__

2 Hey, Lara Are you awake too? I can't sleep whispered Lily

Me neither. I've been awake for hours replied Lara

Picture ____

3 It's some kind of light. But where's it coming from? wondered Lara

Let's go and have a look

Picture ____

4 Lara, come and have a look at this What do you think it is?

Picture ____

4 **Challenge**

Write sentences and dialogues in your notebook for the next two scenes of the story.

5 Spectacular special effects

1 Read

Complete the summary of the *Jurassic Park* film story with words from the box.

> controlled ~~science fiction~~ island dinosaurs
> escape breaks scientists escape dinosaurs

Jurassic Park is a ¹ __science fiction__ film. It is about a group of ² _____ who visit an ³ _____ inhabited by ⁴ _____ . Before the scientists arrive, the dinosaurs live in a ⁵ _____ area on the island and they can't ⁶ _____ . But then, someone ⁷ _____ the security code and the ⁸ _____ escape. The scientists and other people on the island try to ⁹ _____ from the dinosaurs.

2 Why is *Jurassic Park* famous in cinema history? Circle the correct answer.

a It starred lots of famous actors.

b It showed computer generated special effects that were new at the time.

c It is one of the most terrifying films ever made.

3 Read the extract again from the novel, *Jurassic Park* by Michael Crichton. Put the pictures from the story in the correct order.

4 Choose the correct answer.

1 Tina and her parents are at the beach. Her parents are a **next to her**. b **quite far from her**.

2 Tina wants to be a **on her own**. b **with her parents**.

3 Tina a **stays by the sea**. b **moves under the palm trees**.

4 In the sand, she notices a **birds**. b **bird footprints**.

5 Next, she sees a lizard a **coming towards her**. b **running away into the bushes**.

6 The lizard is a **afraid**. b **not afraid of Tina**.

7 Tina thinks that the lizard a **wants to play**. b **wants some food**.

8 The lizard jumps onto Tina's a **hand**. b **toes**.

9 The lizard is a **heavy**. b **not heavy**.

5 Write

Do you think that the creature was really a lizard? Why? Why not? Give at least two reasons to support your answer.

Strategy check! Guess meaning from context

Tick the strategies which will help you to guess meaning from context. Use the strategy to help you with the sentences below.

- Don't read the sentence, just the word, and try to guess it. ☐
- Read the whole sentence to get an idea of the word's meaning. ☐
- Check the dictionary first. ☐

---

6 Word study

Read the sentences from the story. Underline the words that help you understand the meaning of the words in bold.

1 ... Tina decided to move out of the sun, back from the water, to the **shade** of the palm trees.

2 The lizard stood on its **hind** legs, balancing on its thick tail ...

3 ... the lizard jumped onto her hand. Tina could feel its little toes pinching the skin of her **palm** and she felt the surprising **weight** of the animal's body pressing her arm down.

4 And then the lizard **scrambled** up her arm, toward her face.

6 Unit 4 Revision

1 Multiple-choice quiz
Choose the correct word to complete the sentences.

1 _____ are my favourite kind of film – I don't like anything too serious.
   a Dramas   b Comedies   c Historical stories

2 We loved the film – the 3D special effects were _____ amazing.
   a really   b very   c a bit

3 There was a great surprising ending to the film – it was _____ .
   a boring   b thrilling   c slow

4 The _____ watches a film in the cinema.
   a director   b pianist   c audience

5 The first movies were _____ to people in black and white.
   a shown   b showing   c show

6 In 1935, the first film _____ produced in colour.
   a has   b was   c is

7 The _____ of the film is very hard to follow.
   a setting   b costumes   c plot

8 It's a story _____ will make you cry.
   a when   b who   c that

9 'We have to _____ to make sure no-one hears us'.
   a shout   b whisper   d ask

10 *Jurassic Park* is a _____ film about real live dinosaurs in the 20th century.
   a historical   b comedy   c science fiction

11 In the next scene, Tina moved out of the sunlight and under the _____ of the palm trees.
   a cloud   b shade   c sand

50 Cambridge Global English Stage 6 Activity Book Unit 4

My global progress

Think about what you have studied in this unit. Answer the questions below.

1 What topics did you like and why?
   _____
   _____

2 What activities did you like and why?
   _____
   _____

3 What did you find challenging and why?
   _____
   _____

4 What help do you need now?
   _____
   _____

5 What would you like to find out more about?
   _____
   _____

6 What topics and activities relate to other subjects at your school?
   _____
   _____

Cambridge Global English **Stage 6** Activity Book Unit 4

5 Inventions

1 Gadgets

1 Vocabulary Electronic gadgets
Match the words in the box with the pictures. Write the word under the picture.

> tablet
> mini-DVD player
> memory stick
> MP3 player
> ~~camera~~

a _____

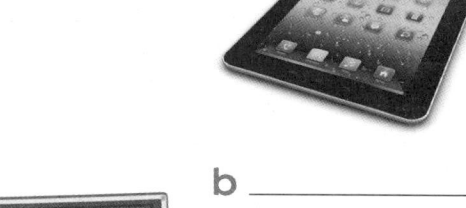

b _____

c ___camera___

d _____

e _____

2 Use the words from Activity 1 to complete the sentences.

1 My favourite gadget has got to be my ___camera___ because I can use it to take photos and make little videos. I take photos of lots of things because I want to be a photographer when I grow up.

2 The most important gadget for me at the moment is this little _____ . I've saved the files for my history project on it and all my holiday photos. I use it on my mum's laptop but this is just for my stuff!

3 I can't live without my _____ because I can store loads of music on it. I've just had some great new headphones for my birthday to go with it.

4 It's got to be my _____ because I can use it to download apps and play games. It's easier to carry around than a laptop and I love the touch screen.

3 **Read** the comments again and answer the questions.

1 Which person finds his gadget useful for storing school work?
2 Which person uses his gadget to do something creative?
3 Which feature does speaker 4 like about his gadget?
4 Which other piece of equipment has speaker 3 got to go with her gadget?

4 **Write**

Complete the phrases about the gadgets that you and your family use.

1 My favourite gadget has got to be …
2 I can use it to …
3 Another gadget that I use a lot is …
4 The most important gadget in my family is …
5 We think it's … than a … because …

a What is your favourite gadget? ☐
b What is the most important reason for using your favourite gadget? ☐
c How many electronic gadgets do you have? ☐

5 **Listen** to Maya talking about her class survey. Tick the question she asked her classmates.

1 Communicate with each other
2 Store information
3 For entertainment
4 Be creative

35% ☐ 15% ☐ 10% ☐ 40% ☐

6 **Listen** again. Use Maya's notes to label the pie chart. Write the numbers of the categories in the correct sections on the chart.

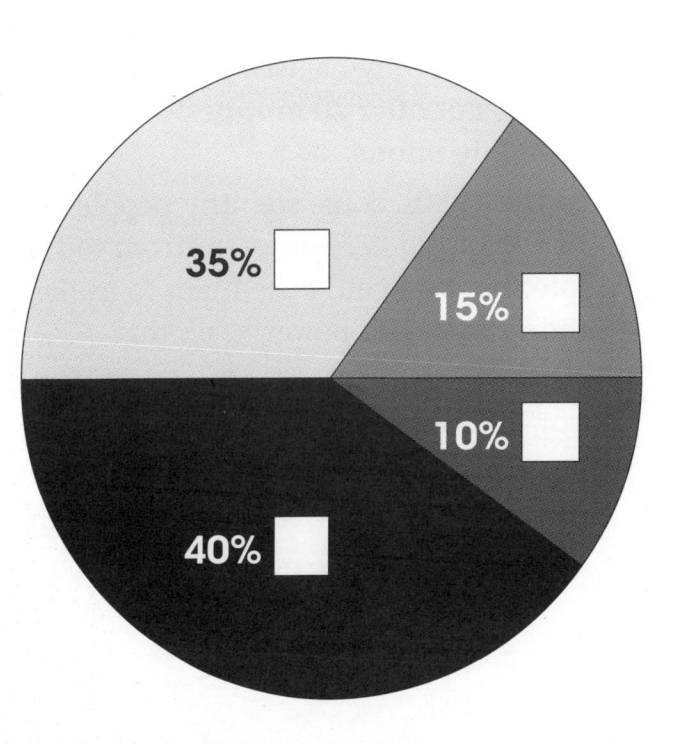

2 Great minds

Strategy check! Use your own knowledge
Tick the strategies which will help you to use your own knowledge to understand a text. Think about what you know about mobile phones before you read the text below.

- Talk about the reading topics first. ☐
- Start reading the text without thinking or talking about it first. ☐

1 **Read** the text and match a picture with a section.

A history of the telephone

1 The telephone has changed a lot over the years. The first telephones were long and tall and used to have a separate mouth and ear piece.   *f*

2 Then, for a long time, home phones had one piece for both listening and speaking. People used to call someone using a round dial.

3 The first 'mobile' phones appeared in the 1970s. They were huge handsets that could only be used in cars. They cost nearly $2000 and the battery used to run out after 20 minutes! At that time only very rich people could afford a mobile phone.

4 In the 1980s, some wealthy people started to carry mobiles. But they were still very big and very different from today's mobiles. They used to weigh nearly a kilo, but you could use them to make international calls. Before this, mobiles didn't have the power to do this.

5 In the early 1990s, mobiles became much lighter; they were known as 'candy-bar' phones because of the slim rectangular shape.

6 Over 30 years later, we have slim, light smart phones with a touch screen and lots of functions. What will be next in the development of the mobile phone?

🇬🇧 mobile phone   🇺🇸 cell phone

2 **Use of English**
Underline four sentences with **used to** in the text.

3 Match the sentence halves to make true sentences about mobile phones.

1 Mobiles didn't use to have
2 Mobiles used to be
3 Mobiles used to weigh
4 People only used to use
5 People didn't use to take
6 Mobiles only used to make

a calls and send texts.
b mobile phones in cars.
c photos with their phones.
d a lot more than they do now.
e too expensive for most people to buy.
f the power to make international calls.

4 Complete the sentences about televisions with the correct form of **use(d) to** and a verb from the box.

own   watch   not change   listen to   ~~not have~~

1 Televisions _didn't use to_ have so many channels.
2 People _____ TV in black and white only.
3 People _____ TV channels with a remote control.
4 _____ your grandparents _____ a TV when they were young?
5 Before TVs, people _____ the radio to hear the news.

> **Use of English**
>
> **Used to for past habits**
> We use **used to** to talk about past habits and states that don't happen now.
> People **used to** light their homes with candles …
> Streets **used to** be dark …
> What **did** people **use to do** before electric light?
> They **didn't use to have** electric light in their homes.

5 Challenge

Answer these questions about you using **used to**.

1 When you were five years old, which toys did you use to play with? When I was five years old I used to play with …
2 Who used to be your best friend when you were very young? Is he/she still your best friend?
3 Have you ever moved house? Where did you use to live?
4 Have you ever changed schools? Which school did you use to go to?
5 What lessons did you use to have when you started school?

3 Bright ideas

1 Use of English

Complete Dmitri's presentation with **will/won't** and a verb from the box.

not have to	make	like	improve
be	do	~~change~~	not get

Use of English

Will for future predictions
This invention **will** change the way people travel ...
People **won't** crash into each other ...
Which idea **will** the judges choose?

A Hello everyone, today I'm going to describe my idea for an invention. It ¹___will change___ the way we do our homework. It ²_____ our school work and exam results too!

B My idea is called the Brain Pen. It is a pen that is powered by your brainwaves. You won't need to hold the pen – you just think about what you want to write and the pen will write it for you. The pen will write as fast or as slowly as you want it to. You ³_____ more relaxed when you do your work because you ⁴_____ write with your own hand!

C The pen will be connected to headphones. The pads on the side of your head will pick up your thoughts; then the words will be transmitted to your pen through a wire and it will write them down.

D This invention ⁵_____ our school work easier because we won't need to worry about writing quickly or neatly. If you have a lot of writing to do, your hand ⁶_____ tired because the Brain Pen will do all the work.

E To sum up, I think both kids and adults ⁷_____ my idea. It will be good for people who write on laptops all the time and find writing by hand too slow. But sometimes you have to write by hand and this ⁸_____ the job for you!

Cambridge Global English Stage 6 Activity Book Unit 5

2 Read the presentation again and match the sections A–E with a heading.

1 Why people need this invention. ____
2 Introduction. __A__
3 How you use the invention. ____
4 A summary of the idea. ____
5 Description of the idea. ____

3 Write

Sort the words to make five questions from Dmitri's audience after his presentation. Answer the questions in your notebook.

1 will / how / mistakes / correct / Brain Pen / the ?
   <u>How will the Brain Pen correct mistakes?</u>

2 handwriting / what / like / will / the / look / ?
   _____

3 wear / will / the / comfortable / headphones / be / to / ?
   _____

4 electricity / will / the / use / pen / ?
   _____

5 will / how / Brain Pen / cost / much / the / ?
   _____

4 Over to you Write two more questions to ask Dmitri about the Brain Pen.

_____
_____

5 Challenge Write about a new invention for your school.

1 Write four future predictions about your school using **will/won't**.

   In 5 years' time my school will ... .

   The teachers probably won't ... .

2 Describe an invention that you think your school will need in the future. Draw a picture to show your idea.

Cambridge Global English **Stage 6 Activity Book Unit 5**   57

4 Changing the world

1 Read

Put the sentences, a–f, in the correct place to complete the essay. Look at the phrases in bold to help you.

¹ _b_ If we didn't have television, we wouldn't know about important things happening in our country or the world. ² ___ **For example**, when we watch the news, we can know what is happening in the next town or on the other side of the world, all in one programme. ³ ___

I think that television is important to educate us and entertain us too. There are educational TV programmes ⁴ ___ Television gives us important information, but it also makes us relax and laugh too. We can watch TV for fun, ⁵ ___ But some people say that families would talk to each other more, if there was no television. **In my opinion**, families can make time for talking and going out and also enjoy watching TV together too. ⁶ ___

a **such as** documentaries about wildlife, history and culture.

b **In my opinion**, one of the most important inventions of all time is the television.

c **This means that** we can know more information about our own country and other countries too.

d **for example**, when we watch cartoons and movies that tell great stories.

e **For these reasons, I think that** TV is one of the most important inventions.

f This is **because** television can bring us pictures and information very quickly and from far away.

2 Use of English

Complete the sentences with the correct form of the verbs in brackets. Use the *Use of English* box to help you.

> **Use of English**
>
> **2nd conditional**
>
> We use the 2nd conditional to talk about situations that are imaginary (not real). 2nd conditional sentences have two parts: **If** + past simple / **would** + verb (without to).
> If we **didn't have** television, we **wouldn't know** about important things ... Families **would talk** to each other more, **if** there was **no** television.

1 If I ___had___ a lot of money, I ___would buy___ a nice big house. (*have / buy*)

2 If my football team _____ the Cup, I _____ with all my friends. (*win / celebrate*)

3 We _____ the Great Wall, if we _____ to China. (*visit / go*)

4 If you _____ live anywhere in the world, where _____ you _____ ? (*can / live*)

5 If we _____ house, we _____ to live in another city. (*move / not want*)

6 If you _____ someone famous, what _____ you _____ them? (*meet / ask*)

3 Write about what you would do if you didn't have the things below.

| television   mobile phone   MP3 player   email |

1 ___If I didn't have a television, I'd read a book.___
_____
_____

4 Challenge

Choose one of the gadgets from Activity 3 and write about why you think it's important. Use the essay on page 58 to help you.

5 Believe in yourself

1 **Read** the extract again from the story, *Start Small, Think Big*. Put the sentences about the story in the correct order.

a Suddenly Garth sees the Barker Boys walking towards him and tries to run away. _____

b Garth feels very excited about testing his new invention – his Umbrella Hat – outside in the street near his home. _1_

c The Barker Boys laugh at Garth and his Umbrella Hat. _____

d The lady has an idea to organise a young inventors' competition for the town. _____

e After talking to the lady, Garth feels much better. _____

f A lady from another house in Garth's street has seen Garth and the boys and asks him if he is alright. _____

g Garth is pleased that his Umbrella Hat protects him against the rain and wind. _____

h Then the lady looks at Garth's Umbrella Hat and likes it a lot. She thinks that it is a clever idea. _____

i Garth feels very upset. Now he thinks that his invention is a failure. _____

j Todd Barker throws the Umbrella Hat on the ground. The boys run away laughing. _____

2 Choose the correct answer.

1 Garth created the Umbrella Hat to
 a **solve a practical problem**.   b **make people laugh**.

2 Garth thinks that his Umbrella Hat is better than a normal umbrella because
 a **it protects you against the rain**.
 b **you don't have to use your hands to carry it**.

3 The lady tells Garth to a **fight back at the boys.**
 b **don't let their attitude stop him from inventing things.**

4 The lady wants to organise a competition to   a **help children like Garth show their clever ideas.**   b **sell children's inventions in her shop.**

3   **Word study** Adverbs
    Change the adjectives into adverbs. Then complete the sentences about the story with the correct adverb.

    > ~~careful~~   quick   secure   rough   gentle

    1 Garth didn't want to damage the hat so he <u>put</u> it _carefully_ on his head.
    2 He fastened it _____ with the strap so it wouldn't fall off in the wind.
    3 When he saw the boys, Garth turned around _____ to run home.
    4 Todd Barker pulled the Umbrella Hat _____ off Garth's head.
    5 The lady took the hat _____ from Garth because she could see it was already damaged.

4   Underline the verbs in Activity 3 that the adverbs describe (number 1 has been done for you).

5   **Pronunciation** Pronouncing 'a'
    Listen and repeat the sentences. Match the sentences which have the same 'a' sound.

    1 *Face* the *day* in a positive *way*!
    2 Don't be *sad* and *mad*, be *happy* and *glad*!
    3 *That* man has *sat* on his *hat*!
    4 You *may* be *crazy*, but you're not *lazy*!

    ### Use of English

    Adverbs
    We use adverbs to describe (give us more information about) the verb in the sentence. Adverbs tell us how something happens.
    You should listen to instructions **carefully** when you're doing a science experiment.
    Adverbs are usually formed by adding **-ly** to an adjective.
    'Are you feeling better now?' she asked gent**ly**.

6   **Values** Believe in yourself
    Imagine you're going to try something new and you're feeling a bit nervous. Tick the attitudes that are the most helpful.

    1 If other kids can do it, so can I!   ☐
    2 If I can't do it, everyone will laugh at me.   ☐
    3 If I don't try, I won't know if I can do it.   ☐
    4 If I fail, I'll feel really bad!   ☐
    5 If I know I've tried my best, I'll feel OK.   ☐

6 Unit 5 Revision

1 **Vocabulary** Gadgets and equipment
Sort the letters and make words to complete the descriptions.

pzsi
olimbe
onpesh
mscsopa
~~ccybisle~~
plsaotp

1 A long time ago, ___bicycles___ used to have a big wheel at the front and a smaller wheel at the back.

2 You use a _____ to tell you which direction you are going.

3 We use _____ to fasten our clothes.

4 Some _____ have touch screens and some have buttons.

5 You can create documents, store files and carry _____ from one place to another.

2 **Use of English**
Use the phrases in the box to complete the sentences.

use to
~~will~~
would (x2)
didn't use to
won't
used to

1 When I'm older, I ___will___ probably live in another city.

2 My sister _____ hate PE, now she loves it.

3 If we could go anywhere in the world, we _____ visit a tropical island.

4 When I was very young, we _____ have homework at school. Homework didn't exist!

5 If I had to choose just one gadget, it _____ be my laptop.

6 He _____ do well in the exam because he doesn't work hard enough.

7 Where did you _____ live when you were very young?

3 **Over to you**
Complete the sentences with your own ideas.

1 When I started learning English, I used to _____

2 When I started school, I didn't use to _____

3 If I could go on holiday tomorrow, I _____

4 In five years' time, my family will probably _____

5 If I could change something in my school, _____

My global progress

Think about what you have studied in this unit. Answer the questions below.

1 What topics did you like and why?
   _____
   _____

2 What activities did you like and why?
   _____
   _____

3 What did you find challenging and why?
   _____
   _____

4 What help do you need now?
   _____
   _____

5 What would you like to find out more about?
   _____
   _____

6 What topics and activities relate to other subjects at your school?
   _____
   _____

Cambridge Global English Stage 6 Activity Book Unit 5

6 Explorers

1 On a mission!

1 **Read** the text on page 65. How did the astronauts' missions benefit other people? Match a heading with a text.

   a Improvements in medicine on Earth. _____

   b Improvements in medicine in space. _____

   c Better communication on Earth. _____

   d More information about Earth's environment. _____

2 Answer the questions about the reasons for the missions. Which space mission …

   a discovered facts about the effects of no gravity? _____

   b helped people all over the world get information more quickly? _____

   c produced important information about the weather? _____

   d helped improve astronauts' health in space? _____

   e produced information that could help fight disease on Earth? _____

   f discovered facts about things like how dirty Earth's air is? _____

3 **Vocabulary** Expeditions
Complete the text with a word from the box.

| ~~mission~~ voyage discover sailed route |

When British yachtswoman, Ellen MacArthur began her voyage in 2005, her [1]___*mission*___ was not [2]_____ to a new land, but to break a world record. She succeeded! She [3]_____ on a [4]_____ which took her through the world's most dangerous seas and broke the world record for the fastest non-stop [5]_____ around the world.

Cambridge Global English Stage 6 Activity Book Unit 6

Women in space

Since 1963, many female space explorers have followed Russian astronaut Valentina Tereshkova. Let's look at the missions of four important female astronauts to find out what astronauts do in space.

1. In **1983**, Sally Ride became the first American woman in space. Her team carried out scientific experiments in space and installed two communications satellites. Satellites make it possible for us to communicate instantly with each other across the world through TV, radio and telephones.

2. In **1984**, Kathryn Sullivan became the first American woman to walk in space. During her mission, she discovered important information about the sun's energy and how it affects the climate in very hot and very cold places on Earth. She also took photographs of Earth and measured air pollution.

3. In **1992**, Mae Jemison became the first African-American woman in space. During her mission, she did scientific experiments using the weightless atmosphere. In space, there is no gravity, so everything floats! Dr Jemison's experiments gave important information about the human body to produce better medicines and healthcare.

4. In **2012**, Liu Yang became the first Chinese woman in space. She did experiments in space medicine, which looks at how astronauts can survive and stay healthy in space. The conditions in space are very hard on the body and space medicine helps astronauts work safely.

2 Exploration exploits

1 **Read** the text. Circle the correct answer below to complete the sentences 1–5.

Ibn Battuta – An amazing journey

Mohammed Ibn Battuta was an extraordinary traveller. In 1325, at the age of 21, he left his home in Morocco in North Africa. He wanted to go on a 16 month pilgrimage*, but instead, he returned nearly 30 years later. During this time, he crossed five continents on foot, by camel and by boat. He was on a mission for knowledge and experience of different kingdoms and cultures. He travelled more than 100,000 kilometres across Africa, the Middle East, Central and South East Asia, China, India and Europe.

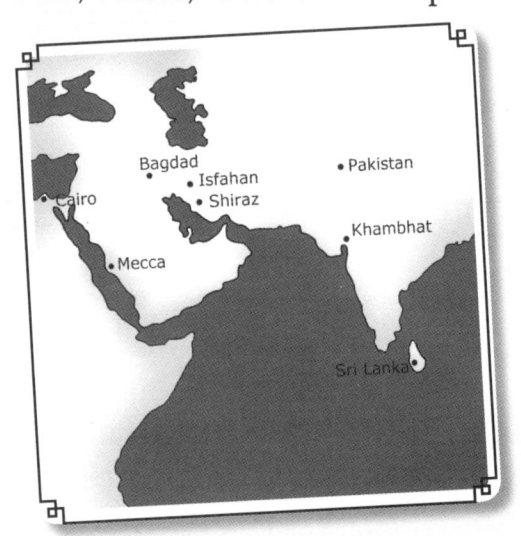

When he returned, Ibn Battuta wrote about his amazing experiences in a book called the *Rihla (Journey)*. His writing shows us a 14th century world that was as international as our world today. He saw people moving between countries to buy and sell goods, share knowledge and make pilgrimages. He wrote about the beauty of exotic cities and the geography of the landscapes. And he noticed how people across continents could be very similar and very different in their habits and customs.

*pilgrimage = a special journey

1 In 1325, **Ibn Battuta was born** / **Ibn Battuta started his travels**.

2 Ibn Battuta was **30 years old when he returned home** / **away from home for 30 years**.

3 Ibn Battuta visited five **continents** / **countries** during his travels.

4 He noticed how people's customs were **never** / **sometimes** the same wherever he travelled.

5 Ibn Battuta lived **after** / **during** the 14th century.

Cambridge Global English Stage 6 Activity Book Unit 6

2 Use of English
Write questions about the text.

1 transport / use / did / what / Ibn Battuta / ?
   What transport did Ibn Battuta use?

2 he / did / many / years / travel / how / for / ?
   _____

3 he / which / travel / continents / in / did / ?
   _____

4 travel / how many / he / did / kilometres / ?
   _____

5 country / which / born / he / was / in / ?
   _____

> **Use of English**
>
> **Question forms**
> Question words + noun
> **How many ships** did Columbus have?
> **What food** did Columbus take?
> **Which countries** did he travel to?

3 Write more questions about expeditions using **question words + noun**.

1 countries / visit _Which countries did the explorers visit?_
2 dangers / face _What dangers did they face?_
3 days / travel for _____
4 things / find _____
5 food / eat _____
6 people / meet _____
7 information / learn _____

4 Vocabulary Exploration
Complete the sentences with a word from the box.

1 Kenya, Ethiopia and Somalia are all on the _continent_ of Africa.
2 The explorers discovered gold and other _____ things.
3 It was an _____ of exploration that lasted four centuries.
4 In the past, expeditions _____ people's knowledge of other cultures.
5 The Aztec _____ stretched across Central America.
6 In the 16th century, the Spanish army _____ the Aztec civilisation.

> valuable
> ~~continent~~
> era
> increased
> empire
> destroyed

3 Intrepid explorers

1 Read Ola and Eva's description of their expedition plan.
Put the paragraphs in the correct order 1–3.

a The ship sank 30 kilometres from the coast here on the map. From this town here, we'll travel by boat until we get to the shipwreck site. We'll need a compass and sea maps to help us sail in the right direction. From here, we'll dive down to explore. As well as our diving equipment – wet suits and oxygen tanks – we'll take underwater cameras. We'll take pictures while we're looking for objects in the shipwreck.

b We're going to go on a diving expedition to the Indian Ocean to explore a 400-year-old shipwreck. This ship had a very bad accident and sank to the bottom of the ocean. We're hoping to find objects that will tell us about the people on the ship and what life was like on board. We'd also like to find out why it sank.

c We'll spend a lot of time on the boat too. As soon as we finish exploring, we'll record our findings on a laptop and upload our photos too. When we're not underwater, we'll need light clothing and also waterproof clothing, in case it rains. There'll be a first-aid kit too, in case we get sick or injured. While we're on the boat, we'll also make a video diary. When we get home, we'll organise an exhibition to show our photos and the objects we found in the shipwreck.

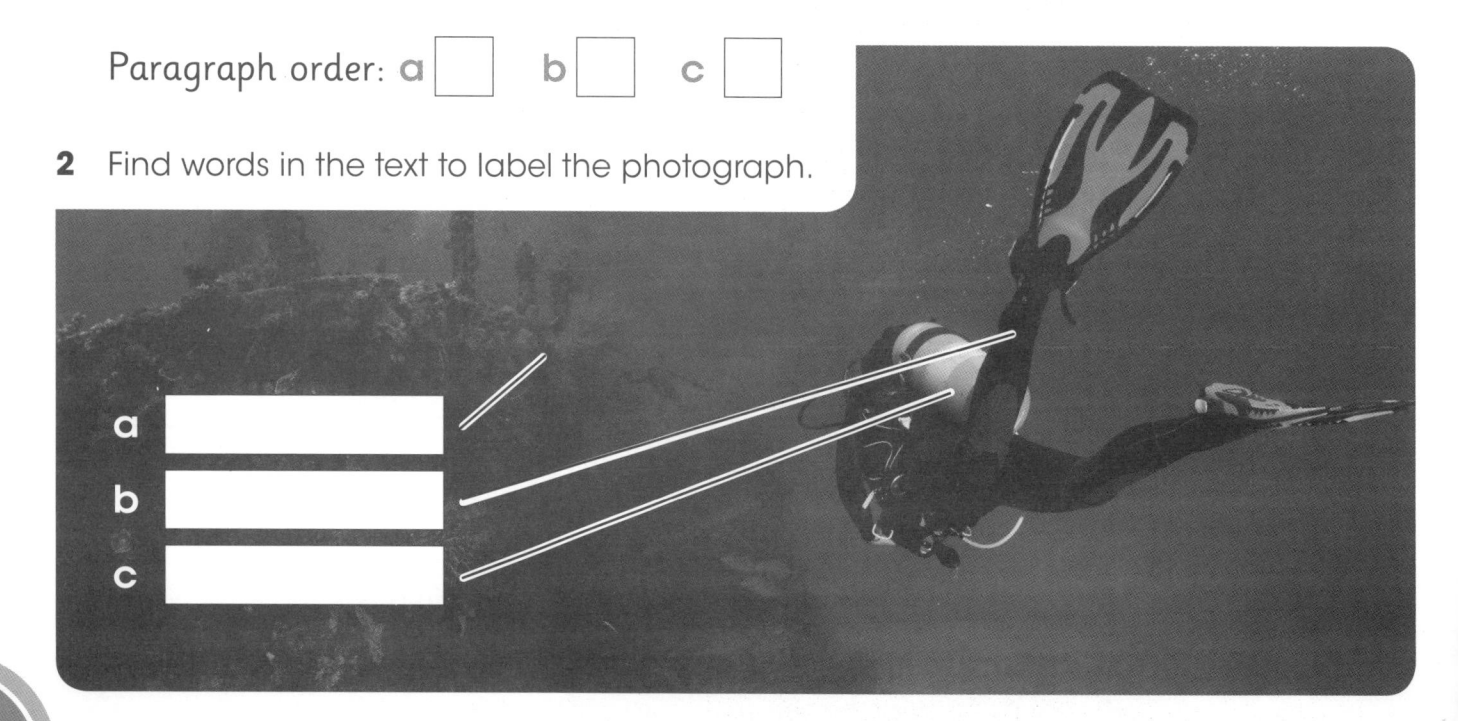

Paragraph order: a ☐ b ☐ c ☐

2 Find words in the text to label the photograph.

3 Read

Circle the answer that is *not* correct.

1 Ola and Eva want to find out about …
   a **life on the ship**.   b **the people on the ship**.
   c **life in the ocean**. ⟵ (circled)

2 While they are underwater, they're going to …
   a **take photos**.   b **make a video diary**.
   c **explore the shipwreck**.

3 While they're on the boat, they're going to …
   a **organise an exhibition**.
   b **make a video diary**.   c **record information**.

4 When they get home, they're going to show people …
   a **a film about the ship**.   b **photos of the ship**.
   c **objects from the ship**.

> ### Use of English
>
> **Linking expressions**
>
> **While, until, as soon as** give information about the time something happens.
>
> We'll take pictures **while** we're looking for objects in the shipwreck.
>
> … we'll travel by boat **until** we get to the shipwreck site.
>
> **As soon as** we finish exploring, we'll record our findings on a laptop.

4 Vocabulary Equipment

Underline ten types of equipment in the text.

5 Use of English

Circle the correct linking expression to complete the sentences.

1 We're going to follow the route **while** / **until** we get to the house. (until circled)

2 We'll make plans for tomorrow **while** / **until** we're having dinner.

3 **As soon as** / **while** they reached the jungle, they knew they needed a map.

4 The rain started **until** / **as soon as** she set up the cameras.

5 We'll keep looking **while** / **until** we see a tiger; then we'll start filming.

6 Complete the plans with **as soon as**, **while** or **until**.

> We're going to take a boat down the river ¹ __until__ we get to the hut. From here we'll trek through the forest ² _____ we find a place to put up our tent. ³ _____ we're putting up the tent, Sam will make dinner. ⁴ _____ we've had dinner, we'll set up the cameras to record nocturnal animals. The camera will record ⁵ _____ we're sleeping. We'll have a look at the film, ⁶ _____ we get up the next morning.

Cambridge Global English Stage 6 Activity Book Unit 6

4 Keeping track

1. **Read** the leaflet for the wildlife park and complete Jack's blog with the times of the activities.

WHITTON WILDLIFE PARK, UK

17 JUNE

What a great day! When we got to the wildlife park at 9.30 am, the first animals we saw from our coach was a group of lions – two males, three females and a cub, which was only four months old. They looked very strong and powerful. Then, at ¹ _____11.00_____ , we went to the orang utan enclosure and watched feeding time. The orang utans were hilarious! They came up close to us and one stole my water bottle!

After lunch at ² _____ , we went to see the sea lion show. The sea lions are so clever and funny. They can understand instructions and do tricks. Next, we went to feed the elephants at ³ _____ . That was fun! The elephants take the food with their trunks and then put it in their mouths. They look strange when you are close to them, but I think they are really interesting. And so huge! Our teacher said that the biggest one was 2.5 metres high and weighed about 3 tonnes.

Then at ⁴ _____ , we saw the bird of prey display. The birds were awesome! We saw falcons, owls and a huge eagle. When it stretched its wings out, it had a wingspan of over 1.5 metres!

This is the second time I've been to this wildlife park and there is always something new to see. I love it!

Have a fun-filled day at **Whitton Wildlife Park!**

11.00	Watch the orang utans at feeding time
12.30	See the sea lion show
13.00	Watch elephants' bath time
13.30	Join the aquarium tour
14.15	Feed the elephants
15.00	See the birds of prey display
18.45	Join the nocturnal animals tour

2 Read the blog again and complete the information.

3 **Use of English**
Read the *Use of English* box. In the blog, circle the ordinal numbers and underline the cardinal numbers in the leaflet.

4 Use the number in brackets and write an ordinal and a cardinal number in the gaps.

1 Today is the ___fifth___ day of the tour and we saw _____ elephants. (5)

2 _____ teachers run the science club at school and it meets on the _____ Wednesday of every month. (2)

3 Bobo is _____ months old. He's the _____ lion born this year. (4)

4 He came _____ in the race out of ten runners. There were _____ other runners who didn't race because they were injured. (3)

5 It's the _____ time we have been to the wildlife park and we've already seen _____ lion and four tigers. (1)

Whitton Wildlife fun facts ...
• Kalu, our oldest elephant measures ¹____ metres from foot to shoulder. He also weighs ²____ tonnes!
• Samson, our largest mountain eagle has a wingspan of ³____ metres.
• Bobo, our newest lion cub is just ⁴____ months old.

Use of English

Numbers
Cardinal numbers tell us the **amount** of something: one, two, three, four, five
Ordinal numbers tell us the **order**: first (1st), second (2nd), third (3rd), fourth (4th), fifth (5th)

70 5 **Pronunciation** Pronouncing numbers
Listen and repeat. What kind of number is pronounced differently?

1 2.15pm   2 6.45pm   3 9.30am   4 2.5 metres

71 6 Pronouncing ordinal and cardinal numbers
Listen and repeat. Circle the number you hear.

1 fourth / four   2 first / third   3 fifth / five   4 sixth / six

7 **Challenge**
Write a blog or diary entry about what you did last weekend. Use time references and dates to organise your work.

Cambridge Global English Stage 6 Activity Book Unit 6

5 Big adventures

1 **Read** the extract again from the novel, *The Boy Who Biked the World*. Decide if the sentences are **T (true)** or **F (false)**. Correct the false sentences.

1 Tom didn't want to go to Abai's house.
<u>False. Tom was very pleased when Abai invited him to his house.</u>

2 Abai's family were very surprised when they saw Tom, but they were pleased to welcome him.
_____

3 There wasn't enough food for Tom as well as all the family.
_____

4 Most of Abai's family could speak English.
_____

5 Abai's Mum served the food with rice. _____

6 The family ate the food by picking it up with the injera bread.
_____

7 Abai showed Tom how to eat the food in the Ethiopian way.
_____

8 Tom said 'thank you' for the food in English.
_____

9 During the meal everyone wanted to find out about each other's countries.
_____

10 Tom learned that the Ethiopian calendar is seven years in front of the rest of the world's calendar.
_____

11 He also learned that, according to Ethiopian time, the day begins when the sun goes down.
_____

12 Abai's family made Tom feel very happy because they were kind to him.
_____

2 **Vocabulary** Descriptive words
Choose the correct word to complete the sentences.

> translated   tore off   ~~chew~~   popped
> scoop up   circular   heaps

1 If you don't __chew__ your food properly, you might get stomach ache.

2 He _____ some paper from the notebook and wrote down his phone number.

3 If I had _____ of money, I would travel around the world.

4 More people could sit around the table because it was a _____ shape.

5 Ana speaks Spanish and English very well, so she _____ the Spanish sentences into English so everyone could understand.

3 **Use of English**
Choose the correct participle adjectives to complete the summary.

At first, Tom was feeling ¹**tiring** / **(tired)** and unhappy because he was missing home. But then he met Abai, who invited him to stay and have dinner with his family. At first Abai's family were very ²**surprised** / **surprising** to see Tom, but they were very ³**pleasing** / **pleased** to welcome him into their home. During dinner, they were ⁴**fascinated** / **fascinating** to hear about his ⁵**excited** / **exciting** adventures and Tom was very ⁶**interested** / **interesting** to find out more about Ethiopia. He was ⁷**surprised** / **surprising** to learn that the Ethiopian calendar is different to the rest of the world. He also thought that Ethiopian food was ⁸**amazed** / **amazing** – it tasted even better because he was so hungry. When he left Abai's family the next morning, he didn't think about the ⁹**tiring** / **tired** journey ahead – he felt ¹⁰**exciting** / **excited** about his adventure once again.

Use of English

Participle adjectives
Participles can often be used as adjectives before nouns or after **be**. Participle adjectives end in **-ing** or **-ed**, according to their meaning in the sentence.

Abai's Mum was **shocked** to learn that people in England do not eat 'injera'.

… Tom was **excited** about his adventure once again.
(excited = Tom's reaction to his adventure)

The food was not always delicious, but it was always **interesting**.
(interesting = the reaction to the food).

4 **Challenge**
Use these participle adjectives in the box to write sentences about you.

> amazing   excited   interesting   tiring   fascinating   surprised   exciting

*The school trip we went on last year was **amazing** because …*

*I always feel **excited** before I go on holiday because …*

Cambridge Global English Stage 6 Activity Book Unit 6

6 Unit 6 Revision

Down ↓

1 _____ island did Columbus find first?

2 During an _____ of about 400 years, European explorers found out many new things about other continents.

3 This word means 'to find out something for the first time'.

7 During the trip, they found a _____ island that was so small, it didn't appear on the map.

9 For any trip, you need to take a first- _____ kit with basic medicines.

Across →

1 We saw two crocodiles __while__ we were going down the river.

4 The first woman in space took part in a 3-day _____ in 1963.

5 As soon _____ they reached the camp, they set up their tents.

6 The night sky was full of bright, _____ stars.

8 The explorers brought back _____ things such as gold and jewellery.

10 He was the _____ person to discover the unknown island.

11 If you build houses on that land, it will _____ the birds' habitat.

2 Challenge
Design your own revision crossword to test your friends.

My global progress

Think about what you have studied in this unit. Answer the questions below.

1 What topics did you like and why?
___
___

2 What activities did you like and why?
___
___

3 What did you find challenging and why?
___
___

4 What help do you need now?
___
___

5 What would you like to find out more about?
___
___

6 What topics and activities relate to other subjects at your school?
___
___

7 Jobs and work

1 Just the job!

1 Read the text about unusual jobs and choose the correct answers below.

Meet two people who do jobs that lots of other people would like to do ...

Lisa Tomas is a chocolate expert. She is fascinated by chocolate and she wants other people to know all about it too. She gives advice to people in hotels and shops about the **best chocolate** to serve and sell to their customers. She also organises events where people can taste **different types** of chocolate.

To do a job like Lisa's, you need to be very knowledgeable about food so that you can give other people **important information** about it. You also need to be good with people and be able to give information to them in a useful and interesting way.

Tom Banks tests **water slides** and rides in **theme parks** for his job. But his fun job has a serious side. He tests the water slides to find out if they are safe for families to use. He looks at the height, speed and amount of water in the slides, as well as other safety aspects. To do a job like this, you need to be good at Maths and Science, so you can understand how things are built and what happens when people use them.

1 Lisa is **quite / very** interested in chocolate.

2 She **gives information about chocolate / sells chocolate** to other people.

3 To do a job like hers, you need to know **how to cook / a lot about** food.

4 In his job, Tom looks for things that can make water slides **dangerous / fun** for families to use.

5 To do Tom's job you need to **build things yourself. / know how other people build things**.

2 Use of English Read the *Use of English* box and underline four examples of **adjectives + prepositions + nouns** in the text.

> **Use of English**
>
> **Adjectives + prepositions + noun**
> Look at these phrases from the listening text. In phrases like this, the adjective and preposition always go together and are followed by a noun.
> I was **good at Maths** and Science anyway.
> I was always really **keen on Science**.

3 Choose the correct preposition. Then complete these sentences to make them true for you.

1 At school, I'm very keen **of** / **on** _____

2 I am fascinated **by** / **in** _____

3 At school, our class works hard **at** / **in** _____

4 Our teacher is very knowledgeable **about** / **in** _____

5 My family is interested **on** / **in** _____

6 Our class is crazy **on** / **about** _____

7 I'm quite good **at** / **of** _____

8 To be a good teacher, I think you need to be good **with** / **on** _____

4 Word study Compound nouns
Look at the words in bold in the text. Which two noun phrases are compound nouns? _____

5 Make five compound nouns out of the words in the word cloud. Which one is the odd one out?

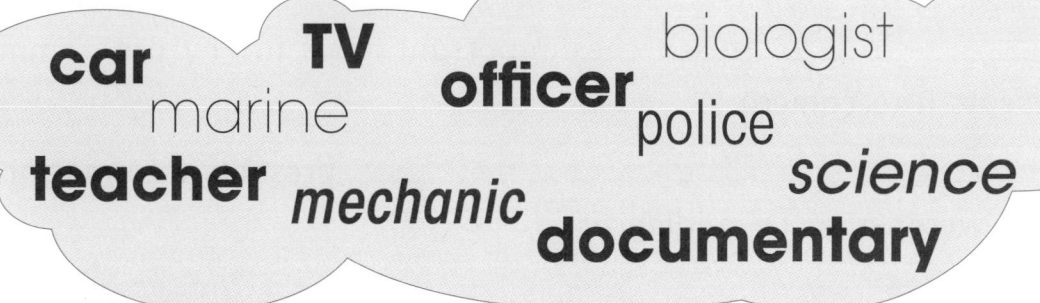

car, TV, officer, biologist, marine, police, teacher, mechanic, science, documentary

6 Challenge

Write a paragraph about a job you are interested in. What skills do you need for it?

I'd like to be a ...   because I'm good at ...   and I'm interested in ...

2 The joy is in the job

1 Vocabulary Personal qualities
Complete the sentences with the correct adjective.

> confident   calm   ~~knowledgeable~~   fascinating   friendly   enthusiastic

1 She is very _knowledgeable_ about history – she knows all the facts.

2 His life is really _____ because he has lived in so many different places.

3 You need to be _____ to give a speech in front of hundreds of people.

4 He didn't get the job because he wasn't _____ about it. He had no energy or interest in it.

5 It's nice to meet such a _____ person – so easy to talk to.

6 He isn't a very _____ person – he panics if there's a problem.

2 Vocabulary Media jobs
Read the definition and write the word.

1 A p r e s e n t e r introduces a TV programme and guides the viewers through the contents.

2 A _ _ _ _ _ _ _ _ _ tells the actors and TV presenters what to do and how to say their lines during the filming of a programme.

3 A _ _ _ _ _ _ _ _   _ _ _ _ _ _ _ _ _ controls the camera that films scenes for TV.

4 A _ _ _ _ _ _ _ _ _ researches important news for TV programmes and presents it to camera.

5 A _ _ _ _ _ _ _ _   _ _ _ _ _ _ _ _ _ _ _ presents information about the weather to TV audiences.

Strategy check! Skimming
Tick the strategies which will help you to skim a text.
- Read quickly first to get the general sense of the whole text. ☐
- Then read the text more slowly to understand the main topic of each paragraph. ☐
- Try to understand all the details the first time you read the text. ☐

Interviewer: Hi, Charlie. Thanks for talking to me today. Can you tell me – what's your job?
Charlie: 1_____
Interviewer: What do you do in your job?
Charlie: 2_____ I go to the scene of the news, find out what's happening and write a short report. Then I stand in front of a film camera and tell the report to TV viewers at home. It's a great job – I love it!
Interviewer: Why do you like it?
Charlie: 3_____ ... and there is always something new to report. Sometimes it's upsetting when I have to report a bad crime, but often there is happy news to report too. I enjoy telling viewers about the good things people do in their communities.
Interviewer: What qualities do you need to do your job?
Charlie: First of all, you need to be knowledgeable about what's happening in your local area. Then you can choose the most interesting and important stories to report. You should also be confident in front of the camera and behind it too. 4_____ To do this well, I need to be confident – not shy! Oh, and you need stay calm if there is a problem on or off air. You can't get nervous if the camera is filming you!

3 **Read** the dialogue and put the sentences, a–d, in the correct place.

a I have to interview lots of different people to find out information.

b I'm a news reporter for a local TV channel.

c It's a fascinating job because news stories are always changing.

d I make news reports about important things happening in my town.

4 **Challenge**

Write a short description of Charlie's job from the dialogue. Use these headings:

Job title   What he does   Why he likes it

What qualities are needed to do the job? Why?

Cambridge Global English Stage 6 Activity Book Unit 7

3 Designing a uniform

1 Vocabulary Clothes and uniforms
Label the picture with words from the box.

| stripe | sleeve | logo | zip | pocket | belt |

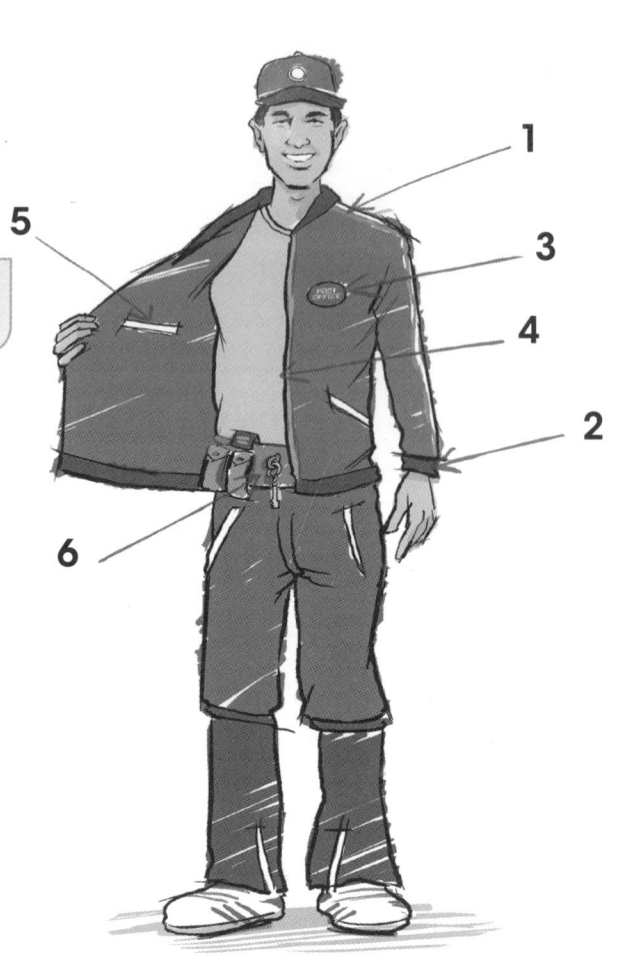

2 Match the sentences with the picture.

a There's a pocket on the inside of the jacket. _____

b The bottom half of the trouser leg is made of waterproof material. _____

c Trainers are comfortable to wear. _____

d The trousers are wide. _____

e There is an alarm in the belt pocket. _____

3 Match the sentence halves with a sentence in Activity 2.

1 ... if you have to walk a lot. ___c___

2 ... to keep money and other small things. _____

3 ... for protection and security. _____

4 ... to protect the trousers from getting wet. _____

5 ... so they are comfortable for people of all sizes. _____

4 **Listen** to Megan talking about her school sports kit. Which is the correct picture?

a   b   c

5 Listen again and correct the underlined word in the sentences.

1 Megan wears the sports kit for <u>basketball.</u>   _running_
2 The tracksuit trousers are light <u>green</u>.   _____
3 The trousers have a white <u>zip</u> down the side.   _____
4 The school logo is on the top <u>left-hand</u> side.   _____
5 She carries a small <u>hand bag</u> when she's running.   _____
6 The tracksuit top has a <u>pocket</u> at the front.   _____

6 Listen to Part 2. Cross out the incorrect word in each sentence.

1 Megan would like to change ~~**the whole sports kit**~~ / **some things only**.
2 Megan thinks the tops should have a **bigger** / **brighter** stripe.
3 Then people can see the runners more clearly when they are **near** / **on** roads.
4 The logo would be better near the **shoulder** / **sleeve**.
5 The backpack needs a pocket **at the side** / **inside**.
6 At the moment, the **backpack** / **water bottle** moves around while she is running.

7 **Challenge**

Design a sports kit for your favourite sport or change the design of a sports kit that you use now. Draw your design and write a paragraph about the different features.

Think about: Style, colour, logo. How practical is your design?
Is it well designed for its purpose?

4 Looking for a job

1 **Read** the first lines of the job advertisements. Match with a picture.

1 We are looking for a hilarious actor to star in our comedy play. _____

2 We are looking for a talented hairdresser to join our creative team. _____

3 We are looking for a dynamic pilot to fly a huge jet plane. _____

2 Match the lines from the rest of the job advertisements with the correct jobs in Activity 1.

1 Must be an expert at using a pair of scissors. _a_

2 Must be knowledgeable about funny books and plays. _____

3 Must know how all the controls in the cockpit work. _____

4 Interviews will be held in the theatre. _____

5 Experience needed – our clients want to look good! _____

6 Must be able to make people laugh a lot. _____

7 Interviews will be held in the cockpit. _____

8 Interviews will be held in the salon. _____

9 Must know how to fly across the world and not go the wrong way. _____

10 Must look good in funny costumes. _____

11 Must have good eyesight so you don't cut the wrong bit. _____

12 Must be good with heights. _____

3 Use of English Read the *Use of English* box. Complete the sentences with the correct form of the verbs in the box.

> not watch   ~~study~~   send
> speak   sell   not sit

> **Use of English**
>
> **Present continuous**
> We use the present continuous to describe continuous actions happening now.
> We **are looking** for enthusiastic and dedicated astronauts ...
> We **are recruiting** genius-level inventors ...

1 Right now my sister _is studying_ for exams.

2 I _____ you this email now – look out for it in your inbox.

3 Which gadgets _____ the most at the moment?

4 We _____ in the garden at the moment, it's too cold.

5 What language _____ you _____ ?

6 I'm _____ TV all evening – I'm going upstairs to read a book.

4 Use the present continuous to write sentences.

1 A school project you're working on at the moment.

2 What's happening in the place you are in right now.

3 A free-time activity you're doing at the moment.

5 Challenge
Complete the job advertisement with your own ideas.

- We are looking for a (adjective) and (adjective) (job title)

- Experience needed – (why?) _____

- Must be good at ... (?) _____

- Must be knowledgeable about ... (?) _____

- Must be interested in ... (?) _____

- Interviews will be held in the ... (where?) _____

Cambridge Global English Stage 6 Activity Book Unit 7   83

5 Achieving a goal

1 **Read** the poem *You can be anything* by Teri Hopkins again.
Tick the sentences that express the advice in the poem.

1 There are lots of different types of jobs that you could do. ✓
2 You can be anything you want to be – you don't have to work hard. ☐
3 It is possible to do any kind of job, but you must make an effort. ☐
4 You should make goals for yourself and aim high. ☐
5 If something goes wrong, you should keep trying. ☐
6 If you are happy in the job you do, you will be successful. ☐
7 Someone else will decide the job you do in the future. ☐
8 You are responsible for choosing the job you do in the future. ☐

2 **Word study** Suffixes
Add **ist**, **er/or**, or **man** to the words for jobs. Then circle the jobs that appear in the poem.

scient _ist_   flor _____   fire fight _____
teach _____   police offic _____   dent _____
build _____   hairdress _____   art _____   doct _____
sing _____   act _____   plaster _____

3 Match a word in Activity 2 with a picture on this page.

a   b   c   d

4 Pronunciation Rhyming sounds

Listen and repeat the rhyming words. Which vowel sounds do you hear?

1 try / sky   2 day / may   3 hair / dare   4 balls / halls

5 Say these words and match the vowel sounds to the sounds in Activity 4. Listen and check.

a calls   b lie   c pay   d care

6 Write a word that rhymes with each word pair in Activity 4.

1 (try / sky) __fly__   2 _____   3 _____   4 _____

7 Use of English

Complete the sentences with **could** or **couldn't** and a verb from the box.

travel   learn   ~~work~~   finish   be   watch

1 If you learn another language, you <u>could work</u> in another country.

2 In a few years' time, she _____ to drive.

3 What do you want to do now?
We _____ TV or play a game.

4 If they stopped messing about, they _____ the work in half the time.

5 If you're good at Science, you _____ a doctor.

6 He _____ on his own – he's too young.

Use of English

could/couldn't (+ verb)

In these sentences, we use **could** (+ verb) to talk about something that is possible.

You **could be** a doctor and look after the sick.

You **could be** a dentist and fix a cracked tooth.

We use **couldn't** (+ verb) to talk about something that isn't possible.

She **couldn't learn** to drive – she's not old enough.

8 Complete the sentences to make them true for you.

1 If I work hard, I _____.

2 When I grow up, I _____.

3 If my family moved house, we could _____.

4 If I finish my homework early, I _____.

5 If me and my friends meet up this weekend, we _____.

6 Unit 7 Revision

1 **Multiple-choice quiz** Choose the correct word to complete the sentences.

1 I'd like to be a _____ when I grow up because I'm interested in engines.
   a police officer   b car mechanic   c vet

2 She was always fascinated _____ the ocean, so she became a marine biologist.
   a about   b in   c by

3 A _____ is a type of media job.
   a florist   b presenter   c doctor

4 You need to be _____ to do a job well – energetic and interested in the work.
   a enthusiastic   b uninterested   c ignorant

5 The opposite of *confident* is _____ .
   a calm   b boring   c shy

6 The _____ tells you which school the team play for.
   a zip   b logo   c waterproof material

7 There are two big _____ on the jacket to keep small things in.
   a sleeves   b logos   c pockets

8 We are _____ for a talented inventor to join our dynamic team.
   a look   b looking   c looked

9 He must be crazy _____ gadgets and machines.
   a about   b with   c on

10 He _____ for any exams at the moment.
   a won't study   b isn't studying   c doesn't study

11 _____ rhymes with *try* or *sky*.
   a why   b way   c we

12 You're good at writing – you _____ be a news reporter.
   a can   b could   c would

86 Cambridge Global English Stage 6 Activity Book Unit 7

My global progress

Think about what you have studied in this unit. Answer the questions below.

1 What topics did you like and why?

2 What activities did you like and why?

3 What did you find challenging and why?

4 What help do you need now?

5 What would you like to find out more about?

6 What topics and activities relate to other subjects at your school?

8 Communication

1 Ways of communicating

1 Vocabulary
Read the comments. Underline six verb/noun phrases which describe ways of communicating.

1. In our class, we have to <u>raise our hands</u> if we want to ask or answer a question. Our teacher tells us off if we call out.

2. My mum always writes notes to remind herself to do things. There are little notes stuck all over the house, especially on the fridge in the kitchen!

3. Last year, I wrote a blog every day when I went on a school trip for a week. Everybody at home could follow it and find out about the great things we were doing every day.

4. I like sending texts to keep in touch with my friends, but sometimes it's quicker to make a call and have a chat.

5. I'm not very good at replying to emails. I forget to check my mail all the time. I prefer sending texts.

2 Over to you
How do you like to communicate? Make five sentences using the verb/noun phrases in Activity 1.

Last term, I wrote a blog about …
I don't like … I prefer …

3 Vocabulary Gestures

Write the words from the box below the pictures.

> a hug   shake your head   make eye contact
> a handshake   wave your hand   a bow   a nod

a ___a handshake___   b _____   c _____

d _____   e _____   f _____   g _____

4 Read

What gestures do people use in your country? Circle the answer that is true for you.

1 When we greet a family member, we often …
   a **hug**.   b **bow**.   c **smile and say hello**.

2 We often greet people we don't know well with …
   a **a bow**.   b **a handshake**.   c **a wave**.

3 When we agree with someone, we …
   a **shake our head**.   b **wave our hand**.   c **nod our head**.

4 When we don't agree with someone, we …
   a **shake our head**.   b **nod our head**.   c **stay quiet**.

5 When we say goodbye to someone, we …
   a **wave our hand**.   b **nod our head**.   c **smile and say good-bye**.

6 In our country, making eye contact is …
   a **OK**.   b **rude**.   c **both – it depends on the situation**.

Cambridge Global English Stage 6 Activity Book Unit 8   89

2 Getting the message

Strategy check! Using key words
Tick the strategies which will help you to identify key words.
- Understand the main topic of the text by looking at pictures, headings, etc; then look for words that link with the topic. ☐
- Look for the words that express the most important information in the text. ☐
- Start reading without looking at any clues around the text and try to understand every word. ☐

1 **Read** Written messages
Read the texts quickly and match with a message type.

> an email   a note   a text message   a shopping list

1 Hi there! We're meeting for <u>pizza</u> on Sat at 2pm – want to <u>join</u> us? Hope to see you there! Lola x

2 Subject: Your birthday
Hello Dan
Thanks for the invitation, but I'm sorry, I can't <u>come</u> to your birthday <u>next</u> <u>weekend</u>. My cousins will be here from Canada and we're having a family celebration on Sunday. Hope to see you soon,
Sam

3 <u>Don't forget!</u> – rice, chicken, beans

4 Please put dish in oven at 5pm. Thanks! See you later.

2 Read the messages again and match with a purpose.

a A reminder. _____
b Asking someone to do something. _____
c An invitation. _____
d Giving information. _____

3 Look at the underlined key words. Underline two more key words in each message.

90 Cambridge Global English Stage 6 Activity Book Unit 8

4 Write

Make messages from the key words.

1 art project / finish / next Fri (Reminder)
   Please remember to finish your art projects by next Friday.

2 Mo's house / football / 5pm / Tues / join us (Invitation)
   _____

3 cinema / can't go / Sat / next week? (Giving information + invitation)
   _____

4 Activities 2, 3 / English homework / Monday. (Instruction from teacher)
   _____

5 Use of English

Read the *Use of English* box. Complete the message with the correct form of the verbs in the box.

| bring | not | come |
| go | ~~meet~~ | have |

Use of English

Present continuous for future arrangements
We use the present continuous to talk about fixed arrangements in the near future.
I'm playing football after school tomorrow.
Dr Singh **isn't seeing** you on Friday …
What **are** you **doing** on Saturday?

Hi Will

Here are the arrangements for my birthday on Saturday at Zany Zoo.
We 1 *are meeting* at the entrance at 10 am. At 10.30 am, we 2 _____ on a special birthday tour of the Reptile House and at 12 pm we 3 _____ lunch at the Iguana café. 4 _____ you _____ your little brother? My cousin 5 _____ any more so there is space for one more.
See you there! Zak

6 Use the present continuous to write sentences.

1 Two arrangements that you have for next week.
   _____

2 Two events that are happening at your school in the next few weeks.
   _____

3 Two arrangements that your family has in the next two weeks.
   _____

3 Explaining something difficult

1 **Read** the conversation between Rupa and her teacher and put the phrases in the correct place.

   a The reason is because ... .

   b Could I talk to you about something?

   c Thanks very much.

   d I need to ask if ... .

   e Would you mind if I ... .

   f I'm sorry, but ... .

Rupa: Excuse me, Mrs Sharma. [1] _b_

Mrs Sharma: Yes, of course, Rupa. What is it?

Rupa: [2] _____ I can change groups for the History project. [3] _____ I'm finding it difficult to work in my group.

Mrs Sharma: Oh ... Why's that?

Rupa: [4] _____ I don't get on well with Nina and Mala. They are always arguing with me. It's causing problems in the group and making us all work slowly. I've tried to talk to them about the problem, but they won't listen. [5] _____ moved to Yasmin's group? They have a spare place.

Mrs Sharma: OK, yes, in this case that's fine, Rupa. Thanks for letting me know.

Rupa: [6] _____ , Mrs Sharma.

---

2 Why does Rupa want to change groups? Choose the correct reason.

   a The History project is too difficult.

   b She has a bad relationship with two other girls in the group.

   c She doesn't like working in Yasmin's group.

3 Use of English
Read the *Use of English* box. Choose the correct word to complete the sentences.

1 Could I **borrow** / **borrowed** your t-shirt?
2 Would you mind if I **give** / **gave** my homework to you on Tuesday?
3 Would you mind if we **didn't** / **don't** stay for the after-school club tonight?
4 Could my sister **joins** / **join** your team?

> **Use of English**
>
> **Polite requests**
> Could I **talk** to you about something? (Polite)
> Would **you mind if** I **handed** it in on Friday instead? (Very polite!)
> After **could**, we use the infinitive; after **Would you mind if** ... we use the past simple.

4 Write the requests again to make them more polite.

1 Can I ask you a big favour? Can I borrow your smart phone later? (*Could* / *Would you mind*)

Could I ask you a big favour? **Would you mind** if I **borrowed** your smart phone?

2 Mr Diaz, can I have a week longer to finish my project? (*would you mind*)
3 Dad, can I ask you something? Can I do my homework on your laptop? (*could* / *Could*)
4 Is it OK if I don't come to football practice tonight? (*Would you mind*)
5 Can you lend me your textbook? (*Could*)

5 Challenge

Use the information in the note to write a dialogue. Make Leah's explanation and request more polite.

Leah: Hi Kate – could I ... ?
Kate: Yes, sure, what is it?
Leah: I'm really sorry, but ... .
Kate: Oh ... Why's that?
Leah: The reason is because ... .
Would you mind if ... ?
Kate: Yes, that's fine, no problem.
Leah: OK, thanks ... .

> Kate, I can't give you back your swimming goggles today. My little brother has broken them. My fault – I let him play with them. Don't worry – my mum is going to buy you a new pair. Can I give you the new ones at the weekend? Leah

4 Getting your point across

1 **Read** the online forum and match with a topic.

   a A school trip that has already happened.

   b How school trips link with school work.

   c Where to go on a school trip.

Teacher: Hi everyone. As you already know, we've got $825 to spend on a school trip. Now I want to hear your suggestions about the kind of trip you would like to go on. Over to you … .

Luisa: Hi everyone. _I think we should_ go on a trip to a historical place because this would help us with next term's history project. **1** [b]

Tiago: Hi Luisa. I think it's a good idea to have a trip linked to school work, but not the History project. How about a trip connected with Science? A lot of kids in our class find Science really hard and need more help with it. _____ **2** [ ]

Maria: _____ But don't you think we need a rest from school work? The school trip should help us relax! What about a trip to a theme park? **3** [ ]

Teacher: Good points so far! Thanks for your comments. What do other people think?

Jose: Hi everyone. Why not do something sporty that no one has done before? _____ rock climbing or canoeing. A sports trip like this would be good exercise and a new experience for everyone. **4** [ ]

Maria: _____ We would have fun and learn something new too. **5** [ ]

---

2 Read the forum again and put the phrases in the correct place.

   a What does everyone else think?   d I see your point, Tiago.

   b ~~I think we should …~~   e Maybe we could go …

   c I agree with Jose.

94 Cambridge Global English **Stage 6** Activity Book Unit 8

3 Which phrases in Activity 2 are used for:

1 introducing your point _____

2 agreeing _____

3 partly agreeing _____

4 encouraging other people to respond _____

5 making a suggestion _____

4 **Read**

Write down four different types of school trip mentioned in the forum and the reasons for each suggestion.

1 A _History_ trip: *to help with the History project next term.*

5 **Calculate** how many students in the class in Activity 1 voted for each idea. There are 30 students in the class.

1 1/2 of the students voted for Jose's idea: _____ students.

2 1/3 of the students voted for Maria's idea: _____ students.

3 1/6 of the students voted for Tiago's idea: _____ students.

4 2/3 of the students would like a 2-day trip: _____ students.

6 **Challenge**

Write a post for an online class forum for two topics from the list. Make a suggestion and the reason why. Write a question at the end that will encourage other students to respond.

- New equipment for your school.
- A new after-school activity at your school.
- A new event for School Sports Day.
- A play or musical for a school production at the end of term.

I think our school needs a new ... for the sports hall because ... .

Maybe we could ... .

What does everyone ... ?

Cambridge Global English Stage 6 Activity Book Unit 8

5 A thank you letter

1 Read the poem *Thank you Letter* by Eric Finney again on page 118 of the Learner's Book. Choose the correct answer to complete the sentences about the poem.

1 The writer thanks the sun for the times it ~~rises~~ / **rises and goes down**.

2 He says that the sun is sometimes **late** / **always on time**.

3 He says that the sun makes grey days **brighter** / **is always behind a cloud**.

4 He thanks the sun for **shining on everyone's face** / **making the whole world feel happy**.

5 He thanks the sun for **burning beaches** / **making beaches hot and bright**.

6 He thanks the sun for **producing fruit** / **making fruit ready to eat**.

7 He thanks the sun for sharing its **heat** / **light**.

8 He says to the sun, 'we know how **valuable you are** / **hot you are**'.

2 Vocabulary Replace the underlined words with a word from the box.

| sunset   ~~blazing~~   ripening   glow   at dawn |

1 The sun is ~~hot and bright~~ today. Don't go outside without a sunhat! _____blazing_____

2 We got up <u>very early in the morning</u> to watch the sun rise. The air felt very warm and fresh. _____

3 The <u>shining light</u> of the sun can be very powerful – take your sunglasses! _____

4 It is early evening now and the <u>sun going down</u> is really beautiful – a fire ball of orange, red and purple. _____

5 The fruit on the tree is <u>becoming ready to eat</u>. Tomorrow we'll pick it and prepare it for dinner. _____

75 **3 Pronunciation**

Listen to the words from the poem. Which sound is the same or similar in each group?

1 dismal / days   2 days / grey / late / slate / wait   3 late / slate / wait

76 **4** Listen to the groups of words. Which sound is the same or similar in each group?

1 funny / face   2 play / day / awake   3 cry / night

4 beautiful / baby / brother

5 Write

Use the matching words in Activity 4 to complete the verse.

Dear baby brother,

Just a line to say,

Thanks for your big smile

And _____ _____ .

You _____ all day,

And _____ at _____ ,

You keep me awake,

But I love you anyway,

My _____ _____ brother …

6 Challenge

Use the guide to write your own short poem about one of the topics below.
Use words that have a similar or matching sound if you can (it doesn't have to rhyme).

Dear …
Just a line to say,
Thanks for (adjective / noun),
And (adjective / noun).
You (verb) …
And (verb) …
My (adjective / adjective / noun)

a person   a place   an animal

Cambridge Global English Stage 6 Activity Book Unit 8   97

6 Unit 8 Revision

1 Vocabulary Read the definitions and complete the words.

1 Write a <u>b</u> <u>l</u> <u>o</u> <u>g</u> : when you write a diary online.

2 _ _ _ _ _ to an email: when you answer an email.

3 _ _ _ _ _ your hand: you do this when you want to answer the teacher's question.

4 _ _ _ _ _ : this verb means 'to say hello'.

5 _ _ _ _ _ your head: in some countries this means 'yes', in others, it means 'no'.

6 _ _ _ _ _ _ : when the sun goes down at the end of the day.

2 Use of English
Complete the email with the correct form of the verbs in the box.

Hi Ben

Can I ask you a big favour? Would you mind if I ¹_____ your football shirt? My shirt has shrunk in the wash – it's now tiny! I ²_____ to football practice tomorrow. It is a very important practice because Mr Jones ³_____ players for the school team. We ⁴_____ at 8 am in the morning. My mum ⁵_____ to the dentist tonight and doesn't have time to buy me a new shirt. If this is OK with you, could I ⁶_____ to your house tonight to pick up the shirt?

Thanks very much, Tom

go (x2)
borrow
come
play
choose

3 Over to you Write sentences and questions for these situations.

1 Ask someone in your family very politely if you can use their laptop to do your homework. _____

2 Make a suggestion for a place to go this weekend with your best friend. _____

3 Write sentences about two arrangements you have for next week after school. _____

Cambridge Global English Stage 6 Activity Book Unit 8

My global progress

Think about what you have studied in this unit. Answer the questions below.

1 What topics did you like and why?
_____
_____

2 What activities did you like and why?
_____
_____

3 What did you find challenging and why?
_____
_____

4 What help do you need now?
_____
_____

5 What would you like to find out more about?
_____
_____

6 What topics and activities relate to other subjects at your school?
_____
_____

9 Travellers' tales

1 Have a go!

1 Vocabulary Holiday activities
Complete the words and match with a picture below.

1 s __ __ f __ __ __   2 __ __ c __ - c __ __ __ b __ __ __
3 __ n __ k __ l __ __   4 b __ __ g __ __ - j __ __ __ __ __
5 __ __ __ w __ __ a __ d __ __   6 __ k __ i __

a
b
c
d
e
f

2 Read the dialogue. Which activities in Activity 1 do the children talk about?

Dina: I'd really like to have a go at snorkelling. It would be fantastic!

Ali: I don't think I'd try it. I don't like deep water.

Dina: You don't have to do it in deep water – you can do it near to the beach – anywhere where there are a lot of fish.

Ali: Mmm, not sure about that. But I'd like to try bungee-jumping. Fantastic!

Dina: So you would jump off a bridge with a piece of elastic around your ankle – but you wouldn't go snorkelling near to the beach! That's weird!

Ali: Yes, I don't mind high places – but I don't like water.

Dina: There's no way I'd go bungee-jumping. I'd be really scared. But I'd like to try skiing. That looks really cool! I've never been to a place where there's lots of snow.

Ali: Me neither. I'd like to try it too.

3 **Read** the dialogue again. Answer the questions.

1 Have the children already tried the activities? _____
2 Which activities would Dina like to try? _____
3 Which activity does Ali think he wouldn't try? _____
4 Which activities would he like to try? _____

> **Use of English**
>
> **2nd conditional review**
> We use the 2nd conditional to talk about imaginary situations (not real). We can use **if** at the beginning of clause or in the second part of the clause. We don't use a comma when **if** comes second.
> **If** I had the chance, I'd like to try skiing.   I'd like to try skiing **if** I had the chance.
> (**If** + past simple), (**would** + infinitive)
> We can use **would** without **if** when we imagine a situation or action:
> I would really like to have a go at snorkelling.

4 **Use of English**
Make sentences from the prompts using the 2nd conditional.

1 Ollie / like / try / snorkelling / if / he / chance
   Ollie would like to try/go snorkelling if he had the chance.
2 Tara's family / like / visit / the Taj Mahal / if they / to India
3 If Luis / have choice / he / go / to Disneyland
4 My uncle / cycle around Europe / if he / have more time
5 If Aisha / go on holiday / she / bungee-jumping

5 **Word study**
Finish the sentences so they are true for you. Use Activity 1 for ideas.

1 I'd like to try _____.
2 I'd really like to have a go at _____.
3 If I had the chance, I would go _____.
4 I don't think I would try _____.
5 There's no way I would go _____.

Cambridge Global English Stage 6 Activity Book Unit 9

2 Where shall we go?

Strategy check! Prediction
Tick the strategies which will help you to guess the content of a reading text.
- Look at what type of text it is by noticing the design and layout. ☐
- Think about the kind of information you can find in specific types of text. ☐
- Read without looking at the design and layout of the text – all texts look the same. ☐

1 Read
What type of text is this? What is it about? Circle the text type.
Then read the texts and answer the questions.

> a news report   an email   reviews in a magazine   a school essay

Planning to go swimming?
Here are our top tips on the best swimming pools around our city.

1 Water Wonder Fun for all the family at this huge indoor swimming pool. Four water slides, wave pool and a toddler fun pool. Swimming lessons and exercise classes too. Quite expensive – almost twice the price of some other pools in the city.

2 Nova Swimming Park Nova has an Olympic-size swimming pool out in the fresh air. Two water slides, diving platform and a little fun pool for toddlers and babies. Good for serious swimmers and fun sessions too for kids on Saturday afternoons (with inflatable rings and toys). Often very crowded on a sunny day. Not cheap, but facilities good.

3 Hampton Baths Small indoor swimming pool in the quiet Hampton neighbourhood. Just the basics here, but nice peaceful atmosphere and friendly pool attendants. No separate pool for young kids. Very clean and good value for money.

4 Wells Lido Part of the beautiful Wells Lake in Russell Park. Only open May to September. A relaxing natural outdoor experience where you might share your swim with some ducks! Family area with a paddling pool and swings for young kids (under 7s not allowed in main pool). Nice and cheap with a good café.

2 **Read** the texts again. Which swimming pool would you recommend for each person?

1 'A small, quiet place, please – not outside …'

2 'We have young kids who like being outside – but we don't want to spend a lot of money.'

3 'I like diving and swimming a long way!'

4 'We have young children who don't want to swim outside.'

5 'I want to do exercises in the pool as well as swim.'

6 'Me and my friends want to play outside in the water – we can only go swimming at the weekend.'

3 Find one negative point about each swimming pool.

_____

_____

4 **Write**
Look at the shortened sentences from the text. Choose a phrase from the box and make full sentences.

1 _There isn't a_ ~~No~~ separate pool
2 _____ fun for all the family
3 _____ two water slides
4 _____ good for serious swimmers
5 _____ not cheap

> It is
> There are
> It isn't
> ~~There isn't a~~
> There is

5 **Over to you** Which swimming pool would you like to go to? Why?

_____

_____

_____

Cambridge Global English Stage 6 Activity Book Unit 9   103

3 Describing a special place

77 **1** **Listen** to Youssef. Put the headings in the order of his description.

   a When Youssef visited Jemaa El-Fna Square ___
   b His feelings about the place. ___
   c Interesting facts about the place. _1_
   d What he saw there. ___

77 **2** **Listen** to Part 1 again. Answer **T (true)** or **F (false)**. Correct the false sentences.

   1 Jemaa El-Fna Square is not known outside Morocco.   T / F
   2 The square has been in movies and on the radio.   T / F
   3 Authors have written about the square in their books.   T / F
   4 Rock stars have made songs there.   T / F

77 **3** **Listen** to Parts 2 and 3. Put the sights in the order that you hear them.

104 Cambridge Global English **Stage 6 Activity Book Unit 9**

4 Use of English

Circle the correct preposition.
Listen to Part 3 again and check.

1 I was fascinated **on** / **by** Jemaa El-Fna square

2 I was really interested **in** / **at** all the food from different parts of my country.

3 I was amazed **about** / **by** the acrobats and musicians.

4 I felt sad **on** / **about** the fact that our trip was so short.

> ### Use of English
>
> **Adjectives + prepositions**
> We often use **prepositions after adjectives** to show how people feel about things.
> I was **surprised by** how fast the time went.

5 Make sentences using adjectives + prepositions. Choose four adjectives from the box and make four sentences for the three topics.

1 a school trip 2 a family trip 3 a special place for you and your friends

On our last school trip, we were surprised by ...

_____

_____

_____

fascinated
sad
amazed
interested
surprised

6 Challenge

Answer the questions about a special place for you. Then write a presentation using your notes. Put the notes into the same order as Youssef's presentation in Activity 1.

1 Think of a place that is special to you. When did you go there? Who did you go with?

2 Write two interesting facts about the place.

3 What did you see there? What were the most interesting sights?

4 How did you feel about what you saw? (Use the adjective + preposition phrases in Activity 5).

4 My dream holiday

1 **Vocabulary** Verbs to describe senses
Label the diagram with the verbs from the box.

touch
hear
smell
taste
see

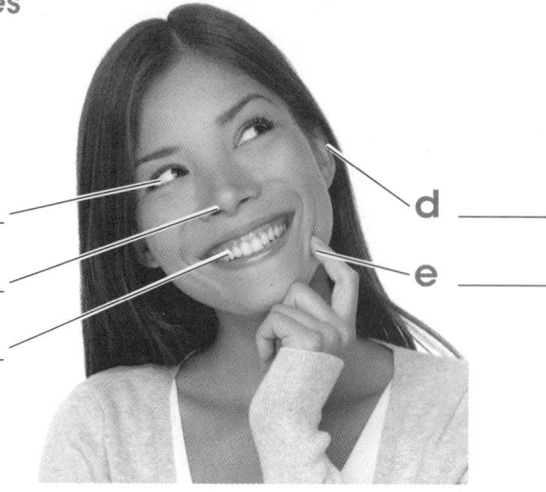

a _____
b _____
c _____
d _____
e _____

2 Complete the poem with the sentences, a–e.
Use the verbs in bold to help you.

If I could travel anywhere in the whole wide world,

I'd travel to Paris in France by train ...

*I'd **see** ¹ d*

*And I'd **hear** ² ____*

*I'd **touch** ³ ____*

*And I'd **taste** ⁴ ____*

*I'd **smell** ⁵ ____*

And then I'd send a private jet for my best friend so she could come too!

a fresh coffee beans in the air.

b people laughing and singing in the cafés.

c warm buttery bread sticks.

d the Eiffel Tower lit up at night,

e the statues in the parks.

3 Vocabulary Descriptive adjectives

Complete the sentences with an adjective from the box.

> shimmering   worn   ~~ancient~~   sapphire   salty

1 The stone statues were ___ancient___ – our teacher said that they were over 2000 years old.

2 They couldn't believe it when they woke up and saw the _____ white sand outside, with the sunlight reflecting off it.

3 _____ sea air is full of oxygen and very healthy.

4 The steps were so _____ that you could easily slip on the stone.

5 The island is famous for its _____ blue waters.

4 Read

Complete Jake's poem with words from the box.

> milkshakes
> friends
> rollercoasters
> slides
> burgers
> pizzas
> laughing
> theme park

If I could travel anywhere in the whole wide world,
I'd fly to a giant [1]_____ ...
I'd see spectacular [2]_____ and rides,
I'd hear people [3]_____ and having fun.
I'd touch the sides as I whizzed down the [4]_____
And I'd taste warm [5]_____ and cold [6]_____
I'd smell the [7]_____ sizzling on the food stalls
And I'd call all my [8]_____ and invite them to join me!

Glossary

sizzling: when you fry something in a pan it makes this sound
whizz: travel very fast

5 Challenge

Write a poem about a place or a country you'd like to visit. Use the poems in Activities 2 and 4 to help you.

Cambridge Global English Stage 6 Activity Book Unit 9

5 Other kinds of journeys

1 **Read** the extract again from the novel, *The Time and Space of Uncle Albert*. Put the sentences about the story in the correct order.

a Gedanken tells Uncle Albert that she hasn't decided on the topic of her science project yet. ___

b Gedanken starts talking to Uncle Albert about her science project. *1*

c Uncle Albert talks about when he tried to 'touch' the stars. ___

d Uncle Albert explains how long it takes for the light from stars to travel to Earth. ___

e Gedanken and her uncle sit down and look at the night sky. ___

f Gedanken asks her uncle how far away the stars are from Earth. ___

2 Choose the correct answer.

1 Gedanken's science teacher wants her class to **find information** / **talk** about a science topic for a project.

2 Uncle Albert thinks the project is funny. Gedanken **agrees** / **is annoyed** with him.

3 Gedanken wants to be a famous scientist like her **uncle** / **teacher**.

4 When he was a little boy, Uncle Albert **knew** / **didn't know** how far away the stars were.

5 Once he climbed up a ladder **at his home** / **in the park** and tried to 'touch' the stars.

6 Uncle Albert tells her how fast light can **travel** / **shine** from the stars to Earth.

7 Gedanken finds this **easy** / **hard** to understand.

Cambridge Global English Stage 6 Activity Book Unit 9

3 **Read** *The speed of light*

Complete the explanation about how light travels. Use the story to help you.

> home   kilometres   Earth   five   room   years   fast   far   ~~night~~

When we look at the stars in the sky at ¹___night___ , the light that we see has taken ²_____ to travel to Earth. This is because the stars are so ³_____ away from ⁴_____ . But light still travels very ⁵_____ at 300,000 ⁶_____ a second! At this speed, light could travel ⁷_____ times around the world in about one second! When we put on a light at ⁸_____ , we don't notice the time it takes for the light to travel from the bulb to fill the ⁹_____ because it is so tiny.

4 **Word study** Expressions with *take*

Complete the sentences and make them true for you.

1 It usually **takes** me _____ to finish my homework.

2 In my country, it **takes** _____ **years** to start and finish school.

3 It **takes** a long **time** to _____ .

4 One subject that I find difficult to **take in** is _____ .

5 It **takes** me **ages** to _____ .

5 **Pronunciation**

Listen and repeat these words from the story. Which sound for the letter 'o' do you hear in each group?

1 topic   long   lost   on

2 so   home   know   ago

6 **Listen** and repeat these words. Match the 'o' sound with groups 1 or 2 in Activity 5.

off __1__   only ____   dome ____   folder ____   project ____   notice ____

7 **Values**

Write down some useful information or advice you have received from one of your family members.

Cambridge Global English **Stage 6 Activity Book Unit 9**

6 Unit 9 Revision

1 Crossword
Complete the sentences with information from each lesson. Solve the puzzle with the missing words.

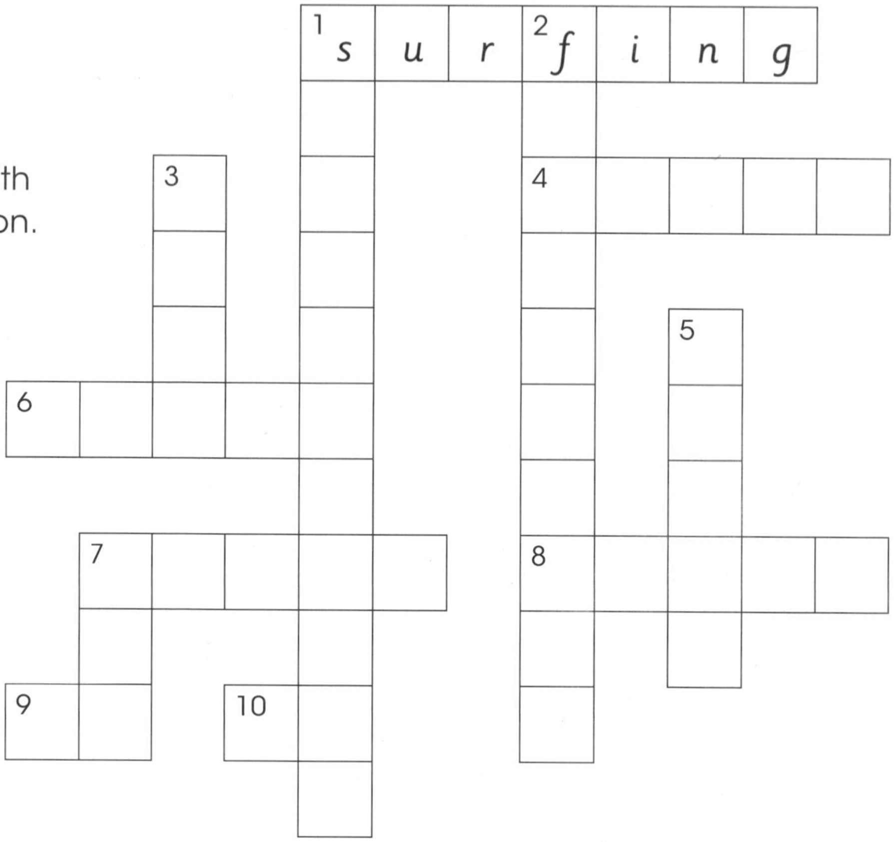

	1 s	u	r	2 f	i	n	g

(crossword grid with squares numbered 1 (surfing across top), 3, 4, 5, 6, 7, 8, 9, 10)

Down ↓

1 When you go _____, you can often see lots of fish in the sea.
2 This word means that you are very interested in something.
3 Was so complicated that we couldn't _____ it in the first time.
5 Hannah felt sad _____ the terrible things that happened in Pompeii.
7 There is no _____ I'd try bungee-jumping!

Across →

1 For this holiday activity you need a board and some big waves.
4 You need your nose to do this.
6 You can find rollercoasters and water slides in a _____ park.
7 If I could try a new activity, I _____ like to try rock-climbing.
8 You do this when you want to feel something with your hands.
9 We were amazed _____ the size of the swimming pool.
10 They visited the museum because they were interested _____ the history of the town.

2 Challenge
Design your own revision crossword to test your friends.

Cambridge Global English Stage 6 Activity Book Unit 9

My global progress

Think about what you have studied in this unit. Answer the questions below.

1 What topics did you like and why?
_____
_____

2 What activities did you like and why?
_____
_____

3 What did you find challenging and why?
_____
_____

4 What help do you need now?
_____
_____

5 What would you like to find out more about?
_____
_____

6 What topics and activities relate to other subjects at your school?
_____
_____

Acknowledgements

Series Editor: Kathryn Harper
Development Editor: Emma Szlachta

Cover artwork: Bill Bolton

The authors and publishers acknowledge the following sources of copyright material and are grateful for the permissions granted. While every effort has been made, it has not always been possible to identify the sources of all the material used, or to trace all copyright holders. If any omissions are brought to our notice, we will be happy to include the appropriate acknowledgements on reprinting.

Photographs
p8 main and background JORGE ADORNO / Reuters / Corbis; p9 2happy / Alamy; p10 Joe Toth / BPI / Corbis; p15 2happy / Alamy; p16 dbimages / Alamy; p30 *t* Aflo Foto Agency / Alamy, *b* George S de Blonsky / Alamy; p31 epa european pressphoto agency b.v. / Alamy; p34 Padmayogini / Shutterstock.com; p41 a Kirill Vorobyev / iStock / Thinkstock, b gferdinandsen / iStock / Thinkstock, c Okea / iStock / Thinkstock, d Ingram Publishing / Thinkstock; p42 Jaguar PS / Shutterstock.com; p44 JEP Celebrity Photos / Alamy; p52 a Oleksiy Kyslenko / iStock / Thinkstock, b Oleksiy Mark / iStock / Thinkstock, c Chiya Li iStock / Thinkstock, d Twister40 / iStock / Thinkstock, e Jorge Juan Pérez Suárez / iStock / Thinkstock; p54 a TimZillionJuan Pérez Suárez iStock / Thinkstock, b Nik_Merkulov / iStock / Thinkstock, c Paul Phillips / Hemera / Thinkstock, d 71gazza / iStock / Thinkstock, e Michael Flippo / iStock / Thinkstock, f Sergej Petrakov / iStock / Thinkstock; p58 Subbotina Anna / Shuttertock; p63 Sergej Petrakov / iStock / Thinkstock; p64 Nigel Hicks / Alamy; p65 1 Photodisc / Thinkstock, 2 Ingram Publishing / Thinkstock, 3 Everett Collection Historical / Alamy, 4 epa european pressphoto agency b.v. / Alamy; p68 vladoskan / istock / T hinkstock; p70 igorkov / istock / Thinkstock; p75 *l-r* Everett Collection Historical / Alamy, Photodisc / Thinkstock, Ingram Publishing / Thinkstock, epa european pressphoto agency b.v. / Alamy; p76 *t* Santje09 / istock / Thinkstock, *b* Maria Pavlova / istock / Thinkstock; p79 claudiaveja / istock / T hinkstock; p87 Santje09 / istock / Thinkstock; p88 *t* skynesher / iStock, *b* skynesher / iStock; p94 Antonius Johannes Slewe / istock / Thinkstock; p99 skynesher / iStock; p104 a David Garry / iStock / Thinkstock, b Goodshoot / Thinkstock, c javarman3 / iStock / Thinkstock, d International Photobank / Alamy; p106 *t* Maridav / iStock / Thinkstock, *b* Alexander Chaikin / Shutterstock.com

t = top
c = centre
b = bottom
l = left
r = right

Development of this publication has made use of the Cambridge English Corpus (CEC). The CEC is a multi-billion word computer database of contemporary spoken and written English. It includes British English, American English and other varieties of English. It also includes the Cambridge Learner Corpus, developed in collaboration with Cambridge English Language Assessment. Cambridge University Press has built up the CEC to provide evidence about language use that helps to produce better language teaching materials.

This product is informed by the English Vocabulary Profile, built as part of English Profile, a collaborative programme designed to enhance the learning, teaching and assessment of English worldwide. Its main funding partners are Cambridge University Press and Cambridge English Language Assessment and its aim is to create a 'profile' for English linked to the Common European Framework of Reference for Languages (CEFR). English Profile outcomes, such as the English Vocabulary Profile, will provide detailed information about the language that learners can be expected to demonstrate at each CEFR level, offering a clear benchmark for learners' proficiency. For more information, please visit www.englishprofile.org